"Building on her seminal work with carnism and powerarchy, in *The Vegan Matrix* Melanie Joy offers another vital treatise that provides crucial guidance for vegan advocates, especially those of us who are privileged. If we truly hope to end oppression, we need to better understand systemic inequity, abuses of power, and embedded traumas experienced by those who are disenfranchised. This cogent book encourages humility, learning, and the radical empathy necessary for healing and for helping to build a powerful vegan movement."—**Gene Baur**, Cofounder and President of Farm Sanctuary and bestselling author of *Farm Sanctuary* and *Living the Farm Sanctuary Life*

"*The Vegan Matrix* offers the ultimate blueprint to empower the vegan movement to become truly inclusive and unified so that we may live up to our core values of universal compassion and respect. This is the big leap on our journey to a vegan world. Every vegan needs to take a deep dive into Melanie Joy's extraordinary work." —**Jane Velez-Mitchell**, Founder of JaneUnchained News Network

"Rather than entrench divisions, Melanie Joy aims to create a stronger movement, literate in the issues of privilege and oppression, and empowered to create change. Everyone looking to transform the world for the better should read this book."—**Leah Garcés**, President of Mercy for Animals and author of *Grilled: Turning Adversaries into Allies to Change the Chicken Industry*

"This book is an easy primer for people to learn about privilege through clear examples, and it provides easy references for people who want to learn more."—**Christopher Sebastian**, author, researcher, and Columbia University lecturer

"*The Vegan Matrix* is practical, focused on impact, and completely accessible to anybody who wants to grow as an advocate and do more for animals. The book provides an outline for how we can lead and communicate effectively to create the strongest movement possible."—**David Coman-Hidy**, President of The Humane League

"This book is a must-read for everyone in the vegan movement and beyond. It has not only helped me question my relationship with my privilege but also opened my eyes to the destructiveness that powerarchy is having on our movement and therefore on our cause: reducing the suffering of animals. *The Vegan Matrix* is a wonderful tool to support us in becoming more effective activists, while at the same time being more compassionate with each other and more unified as a movement."—**Ria Rehberg**, CEO of Veganuary

"This is a very timely, challenging, and convincing book, asking us to deepen and expand our thinking so that we are more effective in our efforts to create a vegan and more compassionate world."
—**Tobias Leenaert**, author of *How to Create a Vegan World*

the vegan matrix

Understanding and Discussing Privilege
Among Vegans to Build a More Inclusive
and Empowered Movement

Melanie Joy, PhD

Lantern Publishing & Media ● Brooklyn, NY

2020
Lantern Publishing & Media
128 Second Place
Brooklyn, NY 11231
www.lanternpm.org

Printed in the United States of America

Library of Congress Cataloging-in-Publication Data

Name: Joy, Melanie, author.
Title: The vegan matrix : understanding and discussing privilege among vegans to build a more inclusive and empowered movement / Melanie Joy, PhD.
Description: New York : Lantern Publishing & Media, [2020] | Includes bibliographical references.
Identifiers: LCCN 2020019940 (print) | LCCN 2020019941 (ebook) | ISBN 9781590566176 (paperback) | ISBN 9781590566183 (ebook)
Subjects: LCSH: Veganism--Social aspects. | Privilege (Social psychology) | Social movements. | Animal rights. | Food animals—Moral and ethical aspects.
Classification: LCC TX392 .J693 2020 (print) | LCC TX392 (ebook) | DDC 613.2/622—dc23
LC record available at https://lccn.loc.gov/2020019940
LC ebook record available at https://lccn.loc.gov/2020019941

For vegans.

Even though you may never be thanked, know that there is great value in your caring; and there is great honor in your courage. Your efforts matter.

Contents

———◇◇◇◇———

Acknowledgments

———◇◇◇◇———

I AM DEEPLY GRATEFUL for the support of the many people who made writing this book possible. I thank my team of compassionate and hardworking change agents at Beyond Carnism for holding down the fort while I was consumed with the writing process, for all the inspiration and cheer they continually provided, for modeling the integrity I write about in this book, and for making sure we always kept laughing: my thanks go to you, Craig Brierly, Ed Startup, Maria Rudden, Tobias Leenaert, Adrian Ramsay—and especially Flavia D'Erasmo, who not only captained our little organizational boat but who convinced me to write this book in the first place. I also thank our Board Chair Dawn Moncrief, a true unsung hero if ever there was one, without whose steadfast and invaluable support this book would no doubt not have been written.

I am deeply grateful for Christopher Sebastian—a brilliant thinker who I'm honored to have as a colleague and a wonderful person who I'm proud to call a friend—for all the time, insights, and support he so generously offered. I am grateful to Ria Rehberg, for being a sounding board and advisor and a dear friend. I also thank my friend and colleague Leah Edgerton, who was involved with this book before I even decided to write it, through brainstorming with me how we might raise awareness of the ideas therein, and for all her support as the writing process unfolded.

As always, I am grateful to the people who make it possible for me to do the work I do to help make the world a better place for animals and vegans: my appreciation goes especially to Jim Greenbaum and Meghan Lowery, two deeply compassionate and justice-minded people for whom I have the utmost respect. I also thank Ari Nessel, for dialoguing with me during the early stages of my writing and helping me hone some of my ideas, and for his wisdom and caring. I thank my editor, Martin Rowe, for being an ally, raising awareness of critical issues in a world very much in need; and I am grateful for Susan Solomon and Kathy Freston, whose friendship is truly a life raft for me. Finally, I thank my husband, Sebastian Joy, who—throughout my multi-book writing process these past three years—kept me fed, laughing, and, above all, feeling loved.

Foreword

David Coman-Hidy, President, The Humane League

———◦◦◦◦◦———

THE MORAL CASE to treat people well, to not harass and abuse our fellow advocates, speaks for itself.

Or, at least, Melanie Joy and others can do a more eloquent job than I can in presenting it. I want to use my space here to reach out to one of the most critical audiences for this book: men (and also people in other positions of power, such as white people) in the animal advocacy movement.

If you're afraid of reading further because you're expecting a treatise or rant or manifesto, fear not. This book is practical, focused on impact, and completely accessible to anybody who wants to grow as an advocate and do more for animals.

Furthermore, if we want to succeed in our shared mission, it's critically important that we—not just men in the movement, but the disproportionately high number of men in leadership positions within animal advocacy organizations—engage with the ideas in this book.

There is a common strain of thinking among self-identified "effective" advocates that I've run across. It worries that a moral panic about issues of gender, class, and other inequities is a distraction from our core issue of preventing animal suffering. People who hold this view (mostly men, but not all) would agree that, for example, sexism is bad, but also fail to see any responsibility to actively *improve* the situation for women or other disadvantaged people in the movement. It's easy to pick out sanctimonious exchanges on social media as examples of how things have gone "too far." Some even point to the major disruption that #metoo caused within the movement as being too costly for animals to have been worth it. But this logic is misguided.

Although the most visible events within the movement were the dramatic derailing of careers, or tense exchanges between leaders and activists, these eruptions are just symptoms of the much more pernicious, chronic impact that patriarchy and other forms of oppression have had on the fight for animals. It is much more difficult to perceive the countless, smaller harms to the cause over the years—such as attrition rates of women leaving the movement, the stunted growth of potential leaders, and the increased hostility and conflict between allied organizations. And all of this has ultimately cost the animals.

The turbulence created by the major #metoo events, paired with the defensiveness of many men and flaring tempers on all sides, has impeded some of the opportunity for growth and healing that the movement so badly needs. Although there are many new policies, there has yet to be a breakthrough in how the movement can collectively discuss and address inequity and inclusion in a healthy way.

What I value about this book, and why I will be recommending it to my colleagues in the movement, is that it focuses on actionable steps for what comes next. It applies concepts most of us are very familiar with from our advocacy to an issue that you may feel much less fluent in. It provides a very accessible primer to understanding the foundational problems, lays out the strategic argument for change, and provides an outline for how we can lead and communicate effectively to create the strongest movement possible.

Introduction

————◦◦◦◦◦————

IF YOU'VE PICKED up this book, chances are you're a vegan and you're all too aware of the devastation that's unfolding every moment as a result of animal agriculture. And chances are you want the suffering and harm to end as quickly as possible. Chances are, too, that ensuring your actions are guided by integrity—practicing the core moral values of compassion and justice—is important to you. So it's likely that even if liberation for nonhuman animals[1] is the focus of your efforts, you nevertheless care about human animals as well, and want to help make the world a better place for everyone. The purpose of this book is to help you improve your ability to do just that.

The Vegan Matrix

In order to help make the world a better place, we need to be aware of the obstacles that may be getting in our way. No matter how well-intentioned we may be, we are only able to consciously act on what we're aware of. Consider, for example, vegetarians who genuinely

---

1 I recognize the value of referring to animals other than humans as "nonhuman animals" or "other animals." However, for clarity and flow—in the interest of keeping the text as reader-friendly as possible—I sometimes use the term *animals*.

care about animals and yet consume vast amounts of cows' milk and cheese because they aren't aware of the brutality of the dairy industry. Or meat eaters who eat "humane" or "organic" animal products, somehow believing they are not contributing to harm. It's as though they were all plugged into a matrix—a machine like that in the movie of the same name that distorts people's perceptions so that they act against their integrity, their own interests, and the interests of others without realizing what they're doing.

Vegans often recognize the particular matrix that shapes people's perceptions when it comes to eating meat, eggs, and dairy, which I refer to as the "carnistic matrix" and which is a byproduct of *carnism*, the oppressive belief system that conditions people to eat animals.[2] We recognize this matrix because, as vegans, we've been unplugged from it. However, the carnistic matrix is but one of many matrices into which we may be plugged, just as carnism is but one of many oppressive systems into which we are born. Each of us has been deeply conditioned within oppressive systems such as sexism, racism, and classism, and our perceptions have been distorted accordingly.[3]

Vegans, like everyone else, are only able to consciously act on what they're aware of. As long as we don't see the matrices that shape our perceptions, we will do their bidding, which may lead us to unknowingly act against our values and the well-being of ourselves, our movement, and the world. The good news is that, with awareness, we can make conscious choices that lead to an all-win scenario: we can more fully practice our integrity, deepen our

2   See Melanie Joy, *Why We Love Dogs, Eat Pigs, and Wear Cows: An Introduction to Carnism* (Newburyport, MA: Conari, 2010, revised 2020).

3   See, for example, E. J. R. David and Annie O. Derthick, *The Psychology of Oppression* (New York: Springer, 2017); Maurianne Adams, et al., (eds.), *Readings for Diversity and Social Justice* (London: Routledge, 2013); and Ana Guinote and Theresa K. Vescio (eds.), *The Social Psychology of Power* (New York: Guilford, 2010).

connections with others and ourselves, and help contribute to a more empowered movement and world.

The Problem of Privilege

About three years ago, in 2017, I realized that a serious problem in the vegan movement, which I had thought was improving, was in some ways worsening. This problem had been (and continues to be) siphoning off a tremendous amount of energy from a movement that needs all the help it can get, while also causing significant suffering among vegans and contributing to harm beyond the vegan movement. This realization, coupled with my belief in the potential of the vegan movement to bring about powerful social transformation and my faith in the integrity of many vegans, brought about the decision to write this book.

It all started—or, more accurately, came to a head—when I was witness to a conversation unfolding on Facebook. It was during the height of #ARMeToo, when multiple charges of sexual harassment had been levied against several esteemed male leaders in the U.S. animal rights movement, catapulting into the vegan spotlight a problem that had long been present but had never been treated with the gravity it deserved. Almost overnight, the veil of denial about sexism was pierced, and for the first time in my three decades in the movement, the issue was being taken seriously and discussed openly. And I was pleasantly surprised to see that the conversation that was unfolding addressed the damage sexism in the movement does not only to women but to people of all genders—and, ultimately, to nonhuman animals.

I (and many of my female colleagues) had tried to talk about *male privilege*—the often-invisible set of advantages given to men and boys at the expense of people of other genders, most obviously girls and women, as a result of sexism—in the movement over the years. But the vast majority of the time, my concerns were responded to in the same way that vegans' concerns are responded to by defensive nonvegans. At best, they were acknowledged but then quickly forgotten. More often, they were reacted to with fervent opposition to me and, likely, to what I represented: a threat to the sexist status quo, the norm. Time and time again, I would raise my concerns—objectively, gently, yet with the urgency I felt they deserved—to find that my efforts to raise awareness were met with resistance, by (mostly) men who were looking at the situation through the matrix of male privilege.

I would point out sexual boundary violations I saw on some of my visits to animal rights organizations, such as male supervisors trying to flirt with their female employees, and be told that I was making a big deal out of nothing. I would point out sexist attitudes, in which men would openly appraise a woman's physical attractiveness—her "youth and beauty"—the way they'd esteem a fancy car and be told that that was just the way men are. I would suggest using nonsexist language or ensuring that girls and women were sufficiently represented in outreach materials, and be told that political correctness was going too far. I would share my personal experiences of sexism with men I thought would understand, to be told my concerns had nothing to do with gender. I would hear men at animal rights conferences calling each other "pussies" and otherwise using feminine terms as a slur, and when I'd point out that this language was offensive I was told that I was overreacting. I would talk about the need for vegans to develop a greater awareness of male privilege (and other forms of privilege, such as white privilege; I'll explain privilege more fully in Chapter 1), and be told that doing so would be a distraction from the "real" issue of animal exploitation.

These arguments were coming not only from independent activists, but from professionals in key positions of leadership in the movement. A number of these professionals were some of the most rational and thoughtful people I knew, whose organizations I'd visited and given trainings for, and who were, like me, highly engaged in assessing and developing strategic vegan outreach— committed to doing the most good possible, as effectively as possible. Yet they didn't realize how failing to address sexism (and other "isms," for that matter, such as racism and classism) in the movement was in many ways fundamentally *un*strategic, hindering the effectiveness of the movement (while also causing harm to vegans and nonvegans alike).

What distressed me perhaps most of all was that I knew that many of the vegan men who refused to take feminism (and other "isms") seriously genuinely cared—about others, their impact on the world, and justice. Of course, we could say the same about the many nonvegans who care and yet refuse to take veganism seriously and continue to eat animals. Indeed, although it's the sexual harassers who carry out overt violations, it's the bystanders who create an environment where such violations are possible, even inevitable—just as the violence of animal agribusinesses is made possible by complicit consumers. One of the great tragedies of oppressive systems such as sexism and carnism (and any social system that's built on power imbalances between groups) is the invisible epidemic of good people who do nothing. It can sometimes hurt more to witness the passive bystanders to injustice than to see the direct perpetrators of it. We expect more from the people we believe in. Perhaps this is why Dr. Martin Luther King, Jr. said that, in the end, it's not the words of our enemies we'll remember, but the silence of our friends.

Adding to my frustration and confusion was the fact that many of the men defending their male privilege admittedly had a very limited understanding of the issue, whereas I had extensive experience to draw on: not only had I been living in a female body for half a century, but I had been active in feminist and other social justice causes for many years. I taught college courses on feminist psychology, violence against women, and privilege and oppression for over a decade; I worked in low-income communities for the 25 years of my teaching career; I had been on the faculty of the Institute for Humane Education, where I was thesis advisor to projects involving the intersection of carnism and other social justice issues; in the early 1990s I was part of the first Boston chapter of Feminists for Animal Rights (FAR); I had been teargassed at anti-globalization rallies and had engaged in civil disobedience in anti-war demonstrations.

But despite the fact that these vegan men and I shared the same values of rationality, compassion, and justice; that I had extensive experience with feminism and other social justice causes; that I was a well-respected strategist in the vegan movement; and that I was a professional communicator, I was unable to cultivate an open, productive dialogue around the issue of sexism (and often other "isms"). I felt like I did when I was a new vegan talking about carnism to nonvegans to whom I just couldn't get through. Indeed, such conversations are not terribly dissimilar; in both cases, they are about privilege, and whatever form it takes—male, carnistic, and so on—privilege causes even the most well-intentioned and thoughtful individuals to resist information that challenges it.

So I literally wept tears of relief after the advent of #ARMeToo, as I read accounts of men (and some women) in the movement who were finally openly engaging with sexism and male privilege as the critical issues they were—and, on top of this, were beginning to see how other "isms" and forms of privilege were similarly problematic. And some of the men who'd previously been resistant to discussing the issue with me were now reaching out to me, asking for more information and expressing their concern over the unjust treatment many women had experienced. It was heartwarming and deeply inspiring for me to witness such a blossoming of awareness.

The Problem of Talking About Privilege

But then something happened. Just a few weeks later, the same men who'd reached out to me with open hearts and minds started again questioning the value of *inclusivity*—of developing an awareness of and sensitivity to sexism and other "isms" (besides speciesism and carnism), and of the privileges that go along with these "isms." Worse, now these men were not only becoming dismissive of the need for inclusivity, but they were starting to feel hostile toward it. They started questioning the need for measures such as developing outreach methods that didn't reinforce the sexual objectification of women or use racist language. Their feelings of protectiveness for the victims of oppression—those who are harmed by privileged behaviors—started to expand toward the offenders.

Confused and deeply concerned, I asked the men about this seemingly sudden shift in their attitudes. They told me they were feeling defensive on behalf of some of the people who had been called out for various infractions—not necessarily for those who had been accused of sexual harassment, but for those whose online comments and questions were being responded to as though the commenters themselves were sexual offenders. As these men witnessed the online conversation unfold, they felt increasingly unsafe and distrustful of those representing feminism and, therefore, of the issue of inclusivity in general.

Of course, as most vegans know, the way an issue is presented doesn't necessarily have anything to do with the value and validity of the issue itself. For instance, just because a vegan engages in demeaning behaviors, such as yelling at and shaming a nonvegan to try to get them to change, this doesn't mean that veganism is not valid and important. But when discussing an issue that people are already defensive against hearing about—such as carnism or sexism—*how* the message is presented matters a great deal. As frustrating and unfair as this may seem, it is simply a psychological reality, and those of us who wish to influence others would do well to relate to those others as they are, rather than as we wish they were.

After learning of the sexual harassment allegations that were revealed during #ARMeToo, men who expressed their distress on behalf of victims were often told that such expressions meant they were selfishly focusing on their own emotions rather than on the needs of the women—whose needs were to be listened to and not spoken to. Men who asked questions to better understand the problem of sexism they were finally starting to acknowledge were often told the same.

To be fair, there were indeed some men who appeared to be responding to the #ARMeToo movement by attempting to sabotage it—angrily demeaning women and defending their male privilege—just as some nonvegans respond to learning about farmed animal exploitation by digging their heels more deeply into defending their carnism. To be fair as well, when people have been trying to talk about an urgent issue—such as sexism or carnism—for years and have been chronically silenced and invalidated, their awareness of and sensitivity to defensive strategies designed to block their message can be acute. Feminists and vegans and others speaking out against widespread injustice may be understandably outraged and have a low tolerance for any communication that reflects resistance to their message. Nevertheless, regardless of whom we're dialoguing with, when we communicate in a way that doesn't honor that person's dignity—that doesn't show we respect their fundamental worth as a being, as equal to our own and to that of all others—even as we may be holding them accountable for their behaviors, we can sabotage virtually any chance of our message being heard. We also send a powerful message to onlookers who may perceive us as unsafe and unjust and, rightly, as reproducing some of the same toxic attitudes and behaviors we're seeking to transform.

So the vegan men who had finally begun to become receptive to the message of feminists (and others speaking about various forms of privilege in the vegan movement) felt like they were in a no-win situation. They told me they had pressing questions, but couldn't ask them without being called sexist (often publicly). They said they wanted to be allies to women and people of other genders, but didn't know what, on a practical level, to do. They admitted that they wanted to educate themselves and become more *literate*—or aware of the issues—but they found the blogs and books about sexism (and in some cases other "isms") often too academic, using language and frames that assumed a base of information they lacked, and sometimes written in a way that seemed to blame more than explain.

About This Book

I wrote this book with two objectives in mind. Both serve the ultimate goals of helping create a more empowered vegan movement and a more just and compassionate world.

First and most importantly, I wanted to present a framework with which to explain a vital issue—the problem of *unexamined privilege* (privilege one is unaware of) and the need for greater inclusivity in the vegan movement—that was tailored especially for vegans who are new to this issue. The issue itself is not new; it has been discussed by a number of others in the movement over the years.[4] This book is not meant to replace those other works, but to complement them, acting as one point of entry into the discussion.

The framework I present in this book uses *carnistic privilege*—a form of privilege to which most vegans can relate, even if they haven't used this particular language to describe it (and which I'll explain more fully in Chapter 1)—in juxtaposition with other forms of privilege. In this framework, I explain not only the problems caused by unexamined privilege, but also the psychology that reflects and reinforces privilege, so that vegans are better able to change their relationship with their privilege and help create a more inclusive movement (and world).

Because with privilege comes power and thus responsibility for how we use that power, and because unexamined privilege has caused (and continues to cause) inestimable harm in the vegan movement and beyond, the primary focus of this book is on raising awareness of privilege. With awareness, those of us in privileged positions are better able to offset the damage that our privilege might otherwise cause.

My second objective for writing this book was to present a framework for communicating about privilege in a way that increases the likelihood that the conversation will lead to positive change and not end up reinforcing dysfunctional communication

---

4   See, for example, Aph Ko and Syl Ko, *Aphro-ism: Essays on Pop Culture, Feminism, and Black Veganism from Two Sisters* (Brooklyn, NY: Lantern, 2017); A. Breeze Harper, "The Sistah Vegan Project: a critical race feminist's journey through the 'post-racial' ethical foodscape . . . and beyond," http://sistahvegan.com; Carol J. Adams, "Carol J. Adams," https://caroljadams.com/blog; Julia Feliz Brueck, *Veganism in an Oppressive World: A Vegans-of-Color Community Project* (Sanctuary Publishers, 2017). Lisa Kemmerer, "Is Sexism Harming Our Activism for Animals?" YouTube, In Defense of Animals, 5 February 2018, https://www.youtube.com/watch?v=K7EZabfOgs4; the work of the Food Empowerment Project, https://foodispower.org/; the work of pattrice jones at VINE Sanctuary, 12 September 2019, http://blog.bravebirds.org/; and the work of Encompass. https://encompassmovement.org/.

patterns and deepening divisions that harm individuals and disempower our movement. This framework is meant to help ensure that discussions about the issue honor the dignity of all involved and provide practical opportunities for change.

I explain why the usual ways of communicating often do not suffice when we're discussing privilege, and present guidelines that can help us communicate more effectively, either when we're communicating from a place of privilege or when we're communicating to challenge privilege. I suggest ways to understand and discuss the issue so that we can talk about abuses of power without abusing power in the process. How we engage with this conversation matters: it can determine whether we create deeper divisions or stronger connections—among ourselves and between our movement and other social justice movements. And it can also determine how we impact the nonhuman animals who are counting on us to be the effective agents of change their lives depend on.

An added benefit to readers is that the communication strategies I share apply to all types of conversations, including those between vegans and nonvegans and between vegans who have different ideologies or strategic approaches. Toxic communication—communication that violates integrity and harms dignity—among vegans is epidemic (as it is among the general population), and healthy, effective communication is a key to personal empowerment and to the empowerment of our movement.

Although this book is about privilege (and oppression, the flipside of privilege, which we'll discuss in Chapter 1) in general, I discuss the issue primarily through the lens of gender, using the circumstances surrounding #ARMeToo as a guiding example. I have chosen to use male privilege as the point of reference in part because the #ARMeToo movement has highlighted and challenged this form of privilege, making the issue more easily understandable for vegans who are new to conversations about privilege and inclusivity. Moreover, as a (white, cisgender, heterosexual) woman, male privilege is one form of privilege I can speak about from extensive experience. Finally, many vegans who are members of various disadvantaged groups other than women have written eloquently about other forms of privilege.[5]

Even though some vegans have already been working to consciously and compassionately promote inclusivity in the movement,[6] for many vegans this is new territory. I believe that the vast majority of vegans can meet this challenge of becoming aware and supportive of inclusivity, as well as of communicating productively, and can work toward the kind of transformation in the movement that they've been working toward in the world. I have met thousands of vegans in my travels, people of integrity who are deeply committed to compassion and justice. And I have seen firsthand the power of those particular vegans who stand up as allies to women and other marginalized people in the movement, vegans who listen with an open mind and heart and who speak out when they notice oppressive attitudes and behaviors.

This book is a call to vegans to play an active role in helping transform the oppressive systems of sexism, racism, and other "isms." For better or worse, we are all a part of these systems. So our choice is not *whether* we participate, but *how* we participate. And no matter how we've participated in the past, every moment offers an

5   See the sources in Footnote 4; also see Christopher Sebastian, "Exploring Connections between Black Liberation and Animal Liberation." YouTube, Vevolutions, 4 March 2017, https://www.youtube.com/watch?v=H_ebX07H4wM; Sunaura Taylor, *Beasts of Burden: Animal and Disability Liberation* (New York: The New Press, 2017); and Anthony J. Nocella II, "Building an Animal Advocacy Movement for Racial and Disability Justice." In *Circles of Compassion: Essays Connecting Issues of Justice*, edited by Will Tuttle (Boston, MA: Vegan Publishers, 2014), 159–169.

6   *Ibid.*

opportunity to change, an opportunity for repair, an opportunity to more fully bring our integrity into the world. Each one of us can choose, right now, to become aware, and to become an active agent of social transformation rather than a passive bystander to injustice. In so doing, we can help heal a deep wound within our movement as well as mend and strengthen our connections with those who work alongside us in the vital struggle for animal liberation.

1

Privilege 101

The Nature of Privilege and the Harm It Can Cause

———◦∞∞◦———

MORE FARMED ANIMALS are slaughtered in a single week than the total number of people killed in all wars throughout human history.[1,2] And the main hope for these animals, at this point in time, is the success of the vegan movement.[3] So farmed animals depend on us, vegan advocates and, by extension, our organizations, to ensure that the movement is as powerful, or empowered, as possible, to lessen and, ultimately, prevent the bloodshed.

Social justice movements such as the vegan movement are more powerful when they are more unified. Being unified is not the same as being uniform. Uniformity is similarity or sameness—of opinions, behaviors, and so on. When we are unified, we feel the sense of connectedness and solidarity that comes, in large part,

---

1   Chris Hedges, *What Every Person Should Know About War* (New York: Free Press, 2003).
2   FAOSTAT, http://www.fao.org/faostat/en/#data/QL. See also Faunalytics, https://faunalytics.org/global-animal-slaughter-statistics-and-charts/.
3   Other strategies to end animal agriculture—such as the development of clean proteins, plant-based health initiatives, and climate targets that include reducing the consumption of animals—are also significant, and they may take on a more important role in the coming years.

from trusting that members of the group are committed to acting in the best interests of one another and of their shared mission. In other words, we trust that they are committed to practicing integrity, which is the integration of values (e.g., compassion and justice) and behaviors. We simply can't feel unified when we don't trust the integrity of those we're interacting with. When a movement is more *internally* unified, there is less infighting and more cooperation among advocates, and when it's more *externally* unified, there's less opposition and more cooperation between the movement and other social justice movements. A unified movement is an empowered movement.

The vegan movement is arguably one of the fastest-growing social justice movements in the world today, and vegan advocates have been doing commendable work advancing the cause. However, there are fractures in the movement through which its power has been leaking, preventing it from achieving the success it otherwise might. Although some vegans had been pointing out these fractures for years,[4] such divisions only started to become visible to the majority of vegans with the advent of #ARMeToo. As explained in the Introduction, several prominent leaders were charged with sexual harassment, opening the floodgates to an outpouring of survivors' stories.

A new awareness among vegans emerged, of the divisiveness and damage caused by unexamined male privilege (and other forms of privilege). However, the dialogue about the issue quickly became heated, with those who identified as feminist (and, to a degree, those who identified as "intersectional vegans") perceived as being in one camp and those who didn't in another. (Vegans who refer to themselves as "intersectional" often use this term to mean that

---

4 See Introduction, Footnote 4.

they recognize that, because all oppressions are interconnected and mutually reinforcing, it's important to become informed about as many oppressions as possible if we wish to help transform them. However, "intersectionality" actually refers to a slightly different phenomenon, which we'll discuss shortly.)

Many vegans who had previously assumed that the ground between them was unbroken—that they shared the same values and beliefs—told me that they'd started to think they were standing on different sides of a chasm. They worried what this divide would mean for themselves, since vegan groups no longer felt like a safe haven from the stressors of the dominant, animal-eating culture, and for the animals whose lives depended on the movement to be unified and empowered. Some also worried that both the problem of sexual harassment in the movement and the ensuing dialogue about the problem were making the movement less attractive to proponents of other social justice movements, whose support they felt was necessary for the vegan movement to eventually achieve popular support.

This chapter is meant to raise awareness of a key cause of the lack of unity in the vegan movement, unexamined privilege among vegans, which is arguably slowing the progress of the movement in a rapidly evolving world. This chapter is also meant to raise awareness of some ways to begin to transcend the problem. With awareness, we can embrace a more progressive veganism, whose approach to understanding and advancing justice for animals is in alignment with the evolving values of a more progressive world. In so doing, we may more swiftly and effectively work toward the transformation of carnism, while at the same time helping to create a better world for all animals, nonhuman and human alike.

Do You Have an Allergic Reaction to the Term *Privilege*?

Privilege is a problem in and of itself. However, the biggest problem with privilege is the damage it does when it's *unexamined*. Unexamined privilege is privilege we are unaware of. Among vegans, unexamined privilege causes us to relate, or interact, in ways that fragment our movement and disconnect us from other social justice movements.

But raising awareness of privilege, which is a necessary step in transforming the problem, is tricky at best. Not only is the concept of privilege widely misunderstood, but our privilege tends to cause us to feel defensive whenever it's discussed. Indeed, many people have an emotional "allergic reaction" to just hearing the term, and are therefore resistant to exploring it further. This is not terribly different from the reasons veganism is tricky to talk about: people are often defensive against the idea of not eating animals; they have misconceptions about what veganism actually is; and they can have an emotional allergic reaction to the word *vegan*. So, to help explain privilege, I've used a specific form of privilege that most vegans can relate to—*carnistic privilege*—as an analogy.

Carnistic Privilege: An Analogy

Most vegans can relate to the frustration, bewilderment, and despair that often accompany discussing veganism with nonvegans. You start out innocently sharing facts about the impact of eating meat, eggs, and dairy on animals, the environment, and human health—facts you're certain the nonvegan will respond to just as you did, just as any rational, compassionate person would. Somehow, though, your words don't land right. The nonvegan isn't getting it, and they're even becoming defensive. Rather than listening openly to you, the expert, they're countering every fact you raise: Their grandfather ate steak every day of his life and lived to the ripe old age of ninety. Their neighbor has always had chickens and those animals have good lives, so what's wrong with eating eggs? Only rich people can afford to be vegan. And so on.

Frustrated, but knowing how critical it is for the animals that you get people to stop eating them, you press on, calmly rephrasing your points in order to be clearer and providing evidence to support them. But no matter how you present the facts, they're perceived as simply your subjective opinion. Bewildered by the irrationality you're witnessing and desperate for your message to be heard, you amplify your claims, highlighting the worst of the abuses, the catastrophic consequences of animal agriculture. To which the nonvegan responds that you're too emotional and you're overreacting; you're exaggerating in order to push a vegan agenda. You're at a stalemate, and you despair, realizing the futility of continuing the conversation.

Most vegans understand, on some level, that the nonvegan is likely behaving in such a way because they're looking at the situation through a distorted lens. The nonvegan has been conditioned by *carnism*, which I explained in the Introduction is an oppressive system that, like all oppressive systems (e.g., racism, classism), creates a particular mentality in those who enable the system and which I compared to being plugged into a machine like that in *The Matrix*. Carnism causes nonvegans to think in ways that support the worldview that eating animals is the right thing to do, so that otherwise rational and compassionate people end up thinking irrationally and acting uncompassionately. This mentality exists in order to keep carnism alive—to defend the practice of eating animals. So it causes nonvegans to feel defensive and to act accordingly whenever they believe their right to eat animals—their carnistic privilege—is being challenged.

Vegans typically know how vital it is to be able to raise awareness in order to transform the oppressive system of carnism. And yet, carnistic privilege—which is designed specifically to prevent the nonvegan from becoming aware, so that they maintain the status quo—can make productive conversation impossible. Carnistic privilege keeps us trapped in a gridlock of defensive debates that fuel our anger, drain our energy, and sap our morale while preventing nonvegans from experiencing the kind of learning and growth necessary for transforming oppression. Nonvegans and vegans often end up pitted against one another rather than uniting to work toward the common goal everyone wants: a more just and compassionate world. In the end, we all lose, including, of course, the animals.

Beyond Carnistic Privilege

A *privilege* is an advantage, practical or psychological, that one person or group has and that is denied to others. Some advantages are earned, such as getting a driver's license when we're old enough and we pass a test. But the kinds of advantages that make up what's commonly referred to as "privilege" are those that are unearned. They're advantages we did nothing to deserve and that were simply given to us because we're members of a dominant social group— the mainstream, or the group that holds the majority of social power. We can, for example, belong to racial, gender, or ideological (e.g., Christian or carnistic) "powerholding" groups, and we are privileged accordingly. For instance, if we're heterosexual we can openly express our affection for our partner without fear of aggression and we can enjoy economic benefits that are denied to individuals of other sexual orientations.

In general, the more privileged groups we belong to, the more social power we have. And all of us belong to both powerholding and nonpowerholding groups: we all, for example, belong to the dominant human group, and even if we appear fully powerholding, we may well have invisible disadvantages, such as a cognitive disability or a psychological disorder.

Some people debate which groups are, in fact, powerholding. Some white people, for example, argue that they experience "reverse racism" and are socially disadvantaged because of their race. However, social scientists can easily determine who holds social power by looking at readily available data sets. Moreover, oppressive systems such as racism or sexism are, by definition, *institutionalized*, meaning that they are embraced and maintained by all major social institutions such as business, medicine, and education. Racism (or any other oppressive system) cannot simply be "reversed," since it's woven through the structure of society via institutionalization. This doesn't mean that white people (and members of other powerholding groups) are never on the receiving end of *prejudice*, which is a preconceived negative opinion about an individual or group. It simply means that members of powerholding groups cannot be oppressed, since oppression is, essentially, prejudice plus power.[5]

One reason privilege is necessary to understand is because of its impact on others. Privilege exists only in relation to others: we can't have an advantage if there's nobody who is at a disadvantage. In other words, if everyone had the same advantage, then it wouldn't be an advantage. For example, as sociologists Stephen McNamee and Robert Miller Jr. point out, if all competitors in a race are given the same head start, then the head start is no longer an advantage.[6]

The flip side of privilege is oppression. Oppression is the experience of being denied advantages that are granted to others. So, just as privileged groups have unfair advantages, oppressed groups have un-

---

5 This definition is derived from that proposed by social scientist Patricia Bidol-Padva in her book *Developing New Perspectives on Race: An Innovative Multi-media Social Studies Curriculum in Racism Awareness for the Secondary Level* (Detroit, MI: New Perspectives on Race, 1970).

6 Stephen J. McNamee and Robert K. Miller Jr., *The Meritocracy Myth* (Lanham, MD: Rowman & Littlefield, 2004).

fair disadvantages. Going back to the example of the race, if some runners are made to start further back in the race due to no fault of their own, they're at an unfair disadvantage. (Of course, the extent and type of disadvantaging is not identical across groups; a BIPOC [Black, indigenous, and person of color], for example, typically experiences far more problematic disadvantaging than does a white vegan.)

The advantages and disadvantages we're granted or denied are not random; they serve a specific purpose. Privileging some people is a key way that systems of oppression remain intact. For example, making some runners start farther back and allowing the others to start farther ahead makes it easier for the privileged runners to win. A system of oppression is like a recurring race that's unfairly rigged: the very same runners keep winning (or losing) and, over time, as the winners are both less fatigued and more confident, the gap between winners and losers grows.

Privilege is a key element that keeps systems of oppression alive. And privilege is the primary reason why the very people who would normally work to transform such systems end up supporting them. Privilege is one of the central factors that prevents logical discussion and maintains widespread injustice and yet, because it's often invisible, many of the people most committed to thinking rationally and acting fairly and compassionately end up doing just the opposite. In other words, without our realizing it, our privilege causes us to defend, rather than challenge, oppression.

The Psychology of Privilege

It can be helpful to think of privilege as an entity that's taken up residence in your psyche, where it needs to remain in order to exist. And it has a survival instinct; your privilege keeps itself alive by keeping you—its host—from recognizing it so it can remain your tenant. This entity has built a fortress in your mind—indeed, it *is* a fortress—that you can't see but that blocks your true awareness. So, unbeknownst to you, you end up looking at the world through the lens of your privilege, which causes you to think, feel, and act in ways that are irrational, unfair, and unkind. But you, being a person who values rational thinking and just, compassionate action, would never willingly nurture such an entity. So your privilege has to trick you into continuing to host it, which it does by distorting your perceptions so that you don't see how it's causing you to make irrational claims, and to act against your moral values and the interests of others.

Also, because you can't see your privilege for what it is, you mistake it for yourself, and *its* feelings become *your* feelings. So whenever someone shines a light on your privilege to help you recognize it, you feel defensive, as if you're personally under attack. The result is that you end up defending the very thing that needs to be evicted from your psyche in order for you to reclaim your authentic thoughts and feelings and be an active agent of social transformation.

All forms of privilege—male, white, carnistic, etc.—share the same defensive psychological structure. The difference is simply the *content* of the privilege, or which oppression it's constructed to defend. So, for vegans, the main difference between carnistic privilege and other forms of privilege is simply that vegans can see carnistic privilege, while they may not see those privileges they possess. Privilege is usually invisible to those who have it; we generally only see the fortress of privilege when we're standing on the other side of it.

Powerarchy: The "Metasystem" of Oppression

All forms of privilege share the same psychological structure because all oppressive systems share the same psychological structure.

It can be helpful to think of oppressive systems as spokes on a wheel. Some of these spokes intersect with one another to create a new category of oppression (as when race and gender overlap, so that Asian women experience a special kind of oppression that is different from that of Asian men or white women), a phenomenon known as *intersectionality*, which was identified by attorney-activist Kimberlé Crenshaw.[7] And a few of these spokes give rise to others, which are offshoots (as when patriarchy—the belief system that values so-called masculine qualities and characteristics over so-called feminine ones—gives rise to sexism, genderism, and heterosexism; racism gives rise to anti-Semitism; or speciesism gives rise to carnism). However, all spokes stem from the same hub: *powerarchy*.[8]

Powerarchy is the term I use for the *metasystem* of oppression, the overarching system that informs all oppressive systems.[9] Powerarchy is organized around the belief in a hierarchy of moral worth, that some individuals or groups are more worthy of moral consideration—of being treated with respect—than others. A powerarchy is a *nonrelational* system, meaning that it reflects and reinforces relational dysfunction—attitudes and behaviors that violate integrity and harm dignity and create disconnection and disempowerment among the individuals in the system.[10]

7   *Intersectionality* was originally intended as a legal term, describing the specific type of discrimination someone faces when they are a member of two or more disadvantaged groups. It can also refer to the distinct type of oppression someone experiences when they belong to more than one disadvantaged group.

8   Melanie Joy, *Powerarchy: Understanding the Psychology of Oppression for Social Transformation* (Oakland, CA: Berrett-Koehler, 2019).

9   Some scholars suggest that racism is the foundation of some other forms of oppression. See, for example, Aph Ko and Syl Ko, *Aphro-ism: Essays on Pop Culture, Feminism, and Black Veganism from Two Sisters* (Brooklyn, NY: Lantern, 2017).

10 Relational-Cultural Theorists have written about nonrelational interpersonal systems and, to a degree, social systems. See Judith V. Jordan, (ed.), *The Power of Connection: Recent Developments in Relational-Cultural Theory* (New York: Routledge, 2010).

Powerarchies are structured to maintain unjust power imbalances between individuals and groups.

Powerarchy also exists on all three relational dimensions: social or collective, interpersonal, and intrapersonal (in our relationship with ourselves through, for example, our inner self-talk and our life choices). The system exists on the "metalevel" (powerarchy is an overarching system), as well as on more concrete levels: carnism and sexism, for example, are powerarchies;[11] as are abusive relationships. Of course, as with all systems, powerarchy exists on a spectrum: a relationship, for instance, can be more or less powerarchical.

To ensure that power remains unfairly distributed, powerarchy uses defense mechanisms so that the participants within the system continue to think, feel, and act in ways that maintain the unjust power imbalance, often without realizing what they're doing. The defenses of powerarchies fall into two (overlapping) categories: myths and privileges. Myths are the stories that validate the powerarchy (e.g., sexism or carnism) and invalidate the counter-system that challenges it (e.g., feminism or veganism). Privileges are the actualizing of the myths, the practices and policies that turn the myths into practical realities—as well as the attitudes and beliefs that go along with these realities. For example, male privilege makes it more likely that men will get paid more than women for doing the same work, and it makes men feel more entitled to being paid more than women.

Although veganism is a counter-system that's structured to challenge the powerarchy of carnism, vegans may nevertheless reinforce other powerarchies, and powerarchy in general, if they are unaware of the existence of powerarchy and of ways that privilege maintains the system. In so doing, they can weaken the vegan

---

11 I use the terms *powerarchy* and *system of oppression* or *oppressive system* interchangeably throughout the book.

movement and contribute to the very mentality they are seeking to transform.

Because powerarchy is nonrelational, driving us to engage in behaviors that create disconnection and disempowerment, a key to transforming powerarchy is learning how to be more relational—developing *relational literacy*, the understanding of and ability to practice healthy ways of relating.[12] You can find resources on powerarchy and relational literacy at the end of this book.

Privilege Literacy

When talking about oppressions such as sexism or carnism, we often get stuck in defensive arguments that end in a stalemate, thus preventing learning, growth, and positive change. People often assume that the reason for such an outcome is because of a difference in values—that, for example, people who eat animals or who oppose developing policies to protect women from sexual harassment have a different value system than do vegans or feminists. Although differing values *may* contribute to the problem (for some people and to some degree), more often the problem is caused not by a difference in values but by a difference in *literacy*.

Whereas linguistic literacy is the ability to recognize letters as well as the ability to understand the meaning of the words they create, *privilege literacy* is knowing the facts about privilege (about the oppression the privilege defends and about the structure of the privilege itself), as well as understanding the meaning of those facts. In other words, privilege literacy is awareness, which is an

---

12 I have written two books to promote relational literacy: *Beyond Beliefs: A Guide to Improving Relationships and Communication for Vegans, Vegetarians, and Meat Eaters* (Brooklyn, NY: Lantern, 2015); and *Getting Relationships Right: How to Build Resilience and Thrive in Life, Love, and Work* (Oakland, CA: Berrett-Koehler, 2020).

intellectual as well as an emotional state. When we are privilege literate, we are informed about the nature and structure of our privilege and we empathize with those who are impacted by it.

Privilege literacy exists on two levels: the metalevel, where we understand the structure and nature of powerarchy and privilege in general; and the specific level, where we understand the facts about a specific powerarchy and the particular form of privilege that defends it. For example, when we are privilege literate in general, we understand the common structures and features of all forms of privilege and systems of oppression, just as an auto mechanic understands the general structure and features of car engines. And when we are literate about a specific form of privilege, we understand the ways that particular privilege gets expressed and the oppressive system it stems from, just as the mechanic understands the unique features of a Volkswagen engine.

The Privilege Literacy Gap

The irony is that although privilege literacy—awareness—is precisely what's needed in order to break the conversational stalemate we so often end up in when trying to talk about oppression, the nature of privilege is such that it prevents those who have it from becoming literate. By its very design, privilege keeps out information that challenges the system the privilege exists to protect, and one key way it does this is by making its "host" believe they are more literate than they actually are.

For example, most nonvegans are far less literate about veganism than vegans are, and yet nonvegans often act as though they're experts on the subject, debating vegans who have spent months, perhaps years, becoming educated about—and experiencing first-hand—their ideology and lifestyle. Similarly, having never taken a single course on gender or learning about patriarchy and how it harms people of all genders, and without any real understanding of the philosophical bases or practices of feminism, some men authoritatively argue that feminism is unnecessary, and is even bad for society.

In both cases, not only is the literacy gap invisible to the individual with privilege, but it is largely their *lack* of literacy that prevents the conversation from moving forward. Were nonvegans to truly understand the horrific impact of carnism—how their minds and hearts have been hijacked by the system, and how their carnistic privilege causes them to act against their core moral values and the interests of others—they would no doubt see vegans as allies rather than opponents. And were men to truly understand 1) the devastating consequences of patriarchy on girls and women, 2) how they have been conditioned to act in ways that harm people of all genders and that cause tremendous damage to relationships, and 3) how their male privilege prevents them from becoming aware of the fact that feminism is, by design, structured to free people of all genders from the violent stranglehold of patriarchy, they would no doubt be allies, rather than opponents, of feminism.

Sometimes, people believe that they are more privilege literate than they actually are because they don't realize that oppression is a bona fide, well-documented phenomenon in the social sciences and they therefore assume that the issue is merely theoretical. There is a vast body of literature, based on extensive empirical research carried out over the course of decades and across cultures and demographics, that describes the key structures of oppressive systems as well as the specific psychological and social mechanisms that reflect and reinforce privilege. In the social sciences, the existence and expressions of these phenomena are generally not up for debate, just as the existence and properties of gravity are not up for debate. Privilege and oppression are factual realities, not simply matters of opinion that we can choose to agree with, or believe in, or not.[13]

Mistaking Facts for Opinions and Opinions for Facts

Another reason why discussions about privilege and oppression can turn into debates and we end up in a stalemate is that our privilege causes us to mistake facts for opinions and opinions for facts. Opinions are subjective, and are therefore subject to debate. Facts, on the other hand, are objective and are therefore not debatable. Without a foundation of facts on which to stand—without an agreement on the basic reality of a situation—a conversation simply cannot move forward.

Consider, for example, how nonvegans often treat the facts you're sharing as "vegan propaganda" and the opinions they're sharing (e.g., "Humane farming doesn't harm animals") as facts. Similarly, I recently spoke with a (white) vegan advocate who had been told their outreach reflected a lack of awareness of racism by a vegan who identified as inclusive—as someone who recognizes that, because all oppressions are interconnected and mutually reinforcing, it's important to become informed about as many of them as possible if we wish to help transform them. However, the first vegan told me that they simply "don't believe in or accept inclusivity."

Changing Our Relationship with Our Privilege

One of the most important things we can do to empower the vegan movement (and to help create a more just and compassionate world)

---

13 See, for example, E. J. R. David and Annie O. Derthick, *The Psychology of Oppression* (New York: Springer, 2017); and Maurianne Adams, et al. (eds.), *Readings for Diversity and Social Justice* (Oxford: Routledge, 2013).

is to change our relationship with our privilege. We can't "get rid" of our privilege, because our privilege is usually not something we choose. Those of us who are white can't just make ourselves Black or brown, and given that we live in a system that advantages those with lighter skin over those with darker skin, we will continue to be granted unfair advantages, whether we want them or not. But we *can* choose to become literate, so that we can become allies in the transformation of oppression rather than defenders of an oppressive status quo. As long as we are not literate, we are likely to stand on the side of oppression, by default. Such is the nature of our resident privilege: we will do its bidding as long as we don't see it for what it is.

How Literate Is Literate Enough?

How do we know if we have a sufficient level of literacy to be able to discuss our privilege productively and relate to it healthfully—so that we're helping to offset, rather than reinforce, oppression? How do we know when requests that we increase our literacy reflect valid needs, rather than defensive attempts to shut down communication? How do we know what sources of information to trust, when there seem to be so many conflicting "facts" about the issue?

It's not possible to determine exactly how literate you need to be to be literate enough, but a decent goal to aim for is the level of understanding you would have if you'd taken a college 101 course on systems of oppression. You should also have at least a basic understanding of the particular form of privilege you intend to explore. For example, if you want to change your relationship with your heterosexual privilege, you should understand the basic structure of oppressive systems and the psychology of privilege, and you should also understand the basic tenets of feminism (the key system that challenges heterosexism) as well as the specific ways heterosexist privilege is expressed. And remember, literacy means both intellectual and emotional awareness—it includes truly understanding *and* empathizing with those who are impacted by your privilege.

You also need to determine which sources of information are credible. There are several ways to do this. First, look for sources by social scientists whose research is peer-reviewed, meaning it's been reviewed and validated by others in academia.[14] Also, look for sources based on research conducted by an established research institute, which can be academic or governmental, such as the U. S. Census Bureau or the United Nations. And look for sources whose motivation, or even simply whose effect, is to decrease, rather than maintain or increase, social power imbalances that enable privilege and oppression. In other words, you should be wary of any source about privilege and oppression that doesn't aim to rectify these problems. Be skeptical of sources that seek to deny, minimize,

---

14 Right-wing critics argue that social sciences departments have a left-wing bias, in part because most faculty in the social sciences identify as left-leaning, or as politically progressive, and in part because of social scientists' general acceptance of systems of oppression as legitimate social phenomena. Such an argument is based on the assumption that social scientists' progressive orientation causes them to believe in the existence of institutionalized power imbalances that unjustly privilege some at the expense of others—that the reason social scientists accept systems of oppression as valid is because they are left-leaning in the first place. However, I believe this assumption reverses cause and effect: it is far more likely that social scientists' understanding of systems of oppression leads them to support progressive politics. Consider, for example, the mathematician and physicist Galileo Galilei, who, following in the footsteps of his predecessor Copernicus, argued against geocentricism (the belief that the other planets and sun revolve around the earth) and for the theory of heliocentrism (the belief that the earth and other planets revolve around the sun). It was not Galileo's progressive orientation that caused him to support heliocentrism, but rather his scientific understanding that led to his progressive orientation. A fundamental difference between left- and right-wing ideologies is that the left recognizes the role of systems in general, and of systems of oppression in particular, in shaping social dynamics. So those with knowledge of such systems will likely support a political orientation that reflects this understanding.

or justify privilege—by claiming, for example, that there is no oppression, or that the situation isn't as harmful as it seems, or that the privileged behavior is normal, natural, or necessary.

One indicator that you are privilege literate enough is that you no longer feel highly defensive when your privilege is justly highlighted—and if you do feel defensive, you realize that it's probably your privilege being activated. (Of course, if you're not being treated respectfully, you'll understandably feel defensive, and we'll discuss this issue in Chapter 4. Nevertheless, it's important to notice when you're feeling defensive, and—to the best of your ability—reflect on your defensiveness to try to determine the cause of it.) Instead, you feel receptive to information about your privilege and are open to modifying your attitudes and behaviors in order to be more of an ally, a person who uses their privilege to offset the oppression it causes.

Another indicator that you're privilege literate enough is that you give the person or persons impacted by your privilege the benefit of the doubt when they share their experience of being disadvantaged. Knowing how powerarchy operates and understanding the psychology of privilege, you realize that the perspective of those without privilege is likely to be more accurate than your own.

Although privilege literacy is essential for everyone, in general, it's more important that a person with privilege becomes literate than does a disadvantaged person, since privilege literacy is usually necessary to offset the defensive distortions caused by privilege. For example, a transgender person doesn't need to have as much privilege literacy around genderism as a cisgender person does in order to discuss genderism effectively, since the transgender person's perceptions and feelings have not been as distorted by cisgender privilege. The times when a disadvantaged person does need to develop privilege literacy are when they feel compelled to defend the privilege that harms them—when, for example, a woman defends male privilege. This kind of defensive behavior typically reflects a psychological phenomenon known as *internalized oppression*, whereby perceptions are distorted in much the same way that they are by privilege, except the perceptions are those of the person negatively impacted by the privilege. For example, *internalized sexism* may be expressed through women engaging in "slut-shaming," degrading other women (or themselves) when they choose to have multiple sexual partners.

I've provided a list of resources for developing privilege literacy at the end of this book that I believe are both accurate and accessible. And in the following chapter, I give an overview of some of the specific ways our privilege affects our perceptions and drives our behaviors, as well as the impact it can have on those with whom we are relating, affecting our interactions both within and outside the vegan movement. This understanding can provide a useful next step toward increasing privilege literacy.

Often, the first step to resolving a problem is recognizing that the problem exists in the first place. So, simply becoming aware of the fact that privilege and oppression among vegans is indeed a problem—and committing to developing privilege literacy to begin to address this issue—is already a move in the right direction, an essential step toward resolution and, ultimately, empowerment.

2
Privilege 201
The Consequences of Unexamined Privilege on Others,
Ourselves, and Our Movement

———◇◇◇———

IN THIS CHAPTER, we'll look at some of the ways our unexamined privilege can affect our perceptions and drive our behaviors, as well as how it can affect those around us. When we become aware of our privilege and its impacts, we're less influenced by it and are better able to make choices that reflect what we authentically think and feel, rather than what our privilege has caused us to think and feel.

Many of the issues discussed in this chapter are well-documented phenomena in the social sciences. Others are based on my own conclusions drawn from my research, my analyses of other research, and my experience doing social justice work over the past twenty-plus years, including my work as a university lecturer on feminism and socialization. Most (though not all) of the examples I've used in this chapter reflect male privilege, for reasons I explained in the Introduction. I've also used a number of personal examples, based on my experience in the vegan movement. However, I've only used personal examples that I know—from observing and speaking with thousands of others—apply well beyond my own experience.

Following are some of the ways our privilege can impact ourselves and others. This list is by no means comprehensive. It simply highlights what I believe are some of the most important features of privilege to be aware of.

Our privilege can cause us to feel like we're more literate than we actually are about the oppression it defends—an issue we touched on in Chapter 1. For example, consider how many times you, a vegan who may have read numerous books and watched countless films about the consequences of eating animals, have been told by nonvegans who've never learned about the issue that egg production isn't as violent as you make it out to be, or that animal protein is necessary for healthy development, and so on.

A similar phenomenon can happen when, for example, women discuss sexism with men. For instance, after speaking as the only woman on an otherwise all-male panel discussing animal agriculture, I commented to my two male (vegan) hosts that the panel discussion reflected a classic gender dynamic: the men interrupted and talked over me every time I spoke. My hosts immediately told me that I was "wrong," and that communication between men and women "doesn't work that way." I asked them how they came to such a conclusion, and they admitted that they knew virtually nothing about patriarchy, feminism, or research on gendered communication, but that they just "didn't believe in feminist arguments." Despite the fact that I had nearly half a century of experience living as a female, that I'd been a professor of feminist psychology, and that I specialized in communication, my hosts felt that their understanding of the issue trumped my own.

Our privilege can make us feel defensive whenever it's highlighted. Our privilege feeds on ignorance, on unawareness—

especially on unawareness of its existence within us. So it can cause us to feel defensive, and to act accordingly, whenever light is shed on it. The irony is that the very thing that would help us change our relationship with our privilege—awareness—is that which our privilege is designed to prevent us from obtaining. Social justice scholars and activists have referred to the phenomenon of being highly defensive against challenges to our privilege as *fragility*.[1] Male fragility, for example, causes men to be especially sensitive to challenges to their male privilege, and what we can call *carnistic fragility* causes nonvegans to be hypersensitive to challenges to their carnistic privilege.

Most vegans are all too familiar with the fact that simply saying they're vegan can elicit a defensive/fragile response from nonvegans, who may immediately start tossing out all sorts of arguments as to why veganism is wrong and eating animals is justified. Indeed, as mentioned previously, nonvegans may have an allergic reaction even to just hearing the term *vegan*. Similarly, if a woman risks admitting that she's a feminist, she can easily end up on the receiving end of a barrage of unsolicited arguments against feminism by some men (and sometimes by women who have bought into the sexist myths about feminism), who have an allergic reaction to the term *feminist*.

Our privilege can make us less rational. Defensiveness is a reaction to a threat, real or perceived. When we feel defensive, we are in a state of *heightened arousal*, meaning that our autonomic nervous system, which controls our fight-or-flight response, is activated, to a greater or lesser degree. In such a state, we have less access to our prefrontal cortex, the part of our brain that's responsible for rational thinking.

---

1   See Robin DiAngelo, "White Fragility," *International Journal of Critical Pedagogy* 3, no. 3 (2011): 54–70.

This automatic response helps keep us alive; it's an instinctive reaction to danger that enables us to immediately deal with a threat. However, it doesn't serve us when what is needed is rational self-reflection.

For example, when confronted with their carnistic privilege, some of the most rational nonvegans may construct elaborate arguments for why eating animals is sensible, by framing veganism as irrational (they suggest that, for instance, veganism is based on subjective emotion rather than rational analyses; or that vegans are biased; or that veganism isn't viable on a global scale; and so on)— arguments which, when analyzed, are themselves irrational.

Further, I was once hired as a consultant by a male leader of a wildlife sanctuary and rehabilitation center, who was concerned with infighting among his team. It turned out that the majority of the conflicts involved women he'd had sexual relationships with, most of whom were much younger than he was and who were distressed because their relationship hadn't ended well. I pointed out the various reasons why having sex with his staff was problematic, not the least of which was due to the imbalance of power between him and them. He replied that he didn't agree with my assessment, because "I didn't ask for this power. I never wanted it." This kind of magical thinking—that simply wishing things were different would make them so—stood in stark contrast to the measured rationality that normally guided this leader's decisions.

Our privilege can cause us to perceive facts as opinions and opinions as facts, an issue we briefly discussed in Chapter 1. Opinions are subjective and are open for debate, whereas facts are objective and are therefore not disputable. But our privilege can cause us to confound these two factors. Consider, for example, how nonvegans often treat the facts you share as opinions and present their own opinions as indisputable facts ("Lobsters don't feel pain;

it's just instinct causing them to scramble to get out of the pot they're being boiled alive in.").

Similarly, I was speaking with a group of vegans when the subject of domestic violence came up and one of the men in the group, who had no experience with or education around domestic violence, insisted that the statistics I was sharing were flawed (I was speaking about how women in heterosexual relationships were more likely to be victims of domestic abuse than were their male counterparts). He claimed that my understanding was wrong, even though I used to teach college courses on the subject and he admittedly had only read some articles online and watched a documentary that touched on the issue.

Our privilege can make us feel that learning about privilege is not important. Oppression—the unjust use of power that privileges some at the expense of others—is arguably the single greatest cause of human-induced suffering on the planet.[2] There is a substantial, scientific body of literature on how oppressive systems operate and on the specific beliefs and behaviors that help maintain the privilege that sustains these systems. Yet, very few people opt to become literate about this highly consequential phenomenon, even though they are inevitably participants in it (we all are). Consider how, despite the fact that universities offer courses on gender and race, and often on oppression in general, many students choose to fill their electives learning, for instance, an ancient language they never intend to use or an instrument they aren't even interested in. And later on, when they're exposed to conversations about privilege, they may argue that it doesn't exist, or that it isn't as problematic as it's made out to be.

---

2   There is significant suffering inherent in nature, such as that among wild animal populations that are not impacted by humans.

A common assumption among vegans is that they don't have to worry about becoming more privilege literate because, out of all privileges, human privilege is the final frontier, and they've already crossed it. This assumption reflects the inaccurate belief that empathy and, by extension, concerns about justice, always develop in a linear and predictable pattern: first, we develop empathy for humans, then for certain animals, then for all animals. It also reflects the assumption that becoming informed about one form of privilege automatically makes us informed about all forms of privilege, which is not the case.

Similarly, **our privilege can make us feel that something is only a problem if we think that it's a problem.** The irony, of course, is that our privilege is designed to prevent us from seeing the problems it causes in the first place. For example, a nonvegan can spend their entire life in denial about the extent of the violence inherent in carnism, even though they may have been exposed to graphic footage of slaughterhouses. Usually, it takes multiple (and often formidable) exposures to the problem to break through the denial caused by carnistic privilege, if the veil of carnistic privilege is pierced at all.

Likewise, it took numerous public allegations of sexual harassment among vegan leaders for vegan women's concerns about pervasive sexist attitudes and behaviors in the movement to finally be taken seriously. Vegan women had been trying to raise awareness of male privilege and the problems it causes for decades, but they remained largely ignored or otherwise invalidated.

Our privilege can make us give more weight to the opinions of those who support it than to those who challenge it. In fact, members of both privileged and oppressed groups all learn to overvalue the opinions of members of privileged groups. For example, vegans, many of whom have critically examined carnism and veganism, can find themselves struggling to hold onto their truth and not second-guess their own opinion when faced with nonvegans who argue that they are overly sensitive, extreme, and so on. And studies have shown that both men and women are more likely to believe men's opinions over women's.[3]

Our privilege can make us feel entitled to never be inconvenienced, and to perceive minor inconveniences as major burdens. For example, consider the nonvegan who claims that the only thing stopping them from becoming vegan is that they can detect a slight difference between a veggie burger and a hamburger. Or consider how people in general, including vegans, often react defensively to being asked to use more respectful language—to avoid, for example, using ableist words such as "deaf." Often, the simple request to change a few words to reflect a growing awareness of, and sensitivity to, oppressive language is met with resistance and offense. Our privilege can cause us to perceive such requests as censorship and to therefore feel unfairly burdened.

Indeed, language offers us a useful window into the dynamics of privilege, since language is a key component in both maintaining and transforming oppression. Words have the power to shape our thoughts, feelings, and consequently, our behaviors. For example, consider how different a nonvegan diner's experience might be if they referred to the chicken on their plate as "someone" rather than "something." And consider how much easier it is to disregard the opinion of an adult when they're referred to as a child, such as when a grown woman is called a "girl."

---

3   See, for example, Sherron B. Kenton, "Speaker Credibility in Persuasive Business Communication: A Model Which Explains Gender Differences," *International Journal of Business Communication* 26, no. 2 (1989): 143–157.

Language evolves as consciousness evolves, and it is therefore dynamic, or ever-changing. Yet many people resist making changes to language—especially changes that limit the power their privilege affords them. Indeed, our privilege can cause us to see any limits on our own control as controlling.[4] People who insist on continuing to use oppressive language often claim that the changes they're being asked to make are going too far (as though there should be some cutoff point where a language stops evolving, and as though deciding what's too far or, rather, far enough, should be determined by anyone other than the group being harmed by the language), because it sounds awkward, or because it's just a word (and if it is truly "just" a word, then changing it shouldn't matter).

Our privilege can make us myopic. When our privilege is challenged, it can cause us to zoom in on our own immediate experience and to fail to see the bigger picture. For example, when vegans present the reasons for not eating animals to nonvegans, some nonvegans focus entirely on the fact that they would feel deprived if they became vegan, disregarding the global catastrophe caused by carnism. And, although discussions about white privilege only began in 1988 when the phrase started to become mainstreamed,[5] whereas racism has existed for millennia, many (white) people complain that talking about white privilege—which makes up just over one percent of the collective conversation—has been going on for too long.

4 This concept is explained by Lundy Bancroft in *Why Does He Do That? Inside the Minds of Angry and Controlling Men* (New York: Berkley Books, 2003).
5 The concept of privilege is believed to have been first published by W. E. B. Du Bois in his book *The Souls of Black Folk* (Chicago: A. C. McClurg & Co., 1903). It was later popularized through Peggy McIntosh's 1988 essay "White Privilege and Male Privilege: A Personal Account of Coming to See Correspondences through Work in Women's Studies," Wellesley, MA: Center for Research on Women, 1988. Available online at https://nationalseedproject.org/Key-SEED-Texts/white-privilege-and-male-privilege.

In a similar vein, **our privilege can make us feel victimized when we hear about the victimization it causes.** For example, when a vegan informs a nonvegan about the violence endured by billions of nonhuman beings in the name of animal agriculture, the nonvegan may respond with anger at the injustice of potentially not being able to exercise their "freedom of choice" when it comes to eating meat, eggs, and dairy.

Likewise, when confronted with their privilege and the suffering it causes, many people feel victimized by not being able to exercise their "freedom of expression." For example, I once had a discussion about sexism in the vegan movement with several male colleagues. After explaining some of the horrific ways patriarchy harms girls and women around the world, often through sexually objectifying and violating them, I brought up my concern about an older male director at an animal rights organization I had recently visited who had commented in front of a group of staff members about how sexy an eighteen-year-old intern's legs looked in her short skirt. (That visit, and the subsequent conversation with my colleagues, took place before #ARMeToo, when most of the vegan men I spoke with, including many of the movement's leaders, didn't believe me when I pointed out that there were inappropriate sexual boundary crossings.) My dinner colleagues responded by saying that the leader's comment didn't seem concerning, and that the intern might have been flattered and appreciated the attention. After I explained why the power imbalance and the sexually objectifying nature of the comment made it inappropriate, my colleagues began complaining angrily about how hard it is to be a man these days, never knowing what the right thing to do is, and saying how unfair it was that they have to be so careful with everything they say. They told me that they found it "infuriating" not to be able to talk about issues without worrying about offending someone.

Although there's no doubt that shifting gender roles is creating confusion and frustration, it's striking that these feelings would trump empathy for the victims of oppression. My colleagues' outrage was directed not at the widespread oppression of girls and women our conversation started out on, but toward the expectation that they try to be more considerate in conversations. Their privilege caused them to feel entitled to say whatever they wanted, whenever and however they wanted to, and to perceive requests to try to communicate more respectfully as an injustice. Moreover, despite the fact that they had apparently been feeling such confusion and frustration around how to relate to women appropriately, none of them had actually tried to get informed in order to make the necessary changes. Even when women, such as myself, had tried to raise their awareness of destructive gendered attitudes and behaviors, rather than listen and learn, they would debate, play devil's advocate, and argue that our supposed gender bias made our points less credible.

Our privilege can cause us to see our needs as more important than the needs of those it disadvantages. For example, some nonvegans will argue that their need to have a traditional meal holds more weight than a vegan's need to actually be able to eat the meal, so the nonvegan won't, for instance, swap the butter for margarine in the mashed potatoes they're preparing. Similarly, some vegans who have been criticized in a less-than-ideal manner for using oppressive language or insensitive outreach strategies refuse to become privilege literate and change such behaviors because they don't want to "give in to pressure" or because learning about the issue has become "too triggering." These vegans feel that their need not to feel uncomfortable trumps the need of the group their communications and outreach are impacting not to be harmed.

*

Our privilege can make us feel entitled to dismiss or ignore an entire movement, issue, or concept, based simply on our personal, anecdotal experience. For example, consider the nonvegan who rejects all things vegan because they'd been confronted by aggressive vegans who turned them off to the cause. Or consider the vegan who refuses to examine their white privilege because they'd been confronted by aggressive anti-racism advocates who turned them off to the issue. Or consider the man who says he doesn't believe women have less social power because he comes from a family of strong women or because he's been unsuccessful in the dating world so, according to his analysis, women have more power than men.

Our privilege can distort our perceptions of anger. Because anger, which is the emotional reaction to unjust attitudes and behaviors, drives people to challenge injustice, it is a threat to systems that are based on injustice. So when someone who challenges a system of oppression or the privilege that upholds it expresses anger, those of us with privilege often perceive this anger as more intense than it actually is. Furthermore, we tend to perceive the individual as "an angry person," rather than as "a person who is angry," which distracts us from the real issue by causing us to focus on a supposed internal personal problem with the individual, rather than on the external social problem they're angry about.

Consider how vegan advocates are often perceived as angry, even when they're communicating calmly and compassionately. Or how, when women discuss sexism, the slightest hint of anger is often seen as an aggressive attack and the women are labeled "bitches" or worse, making their anger seem like it's an unhealthy aspect of their character rather than a legitimate emotional response to the injustice of patriarchy.

*

Similarly, **our privilege can make us feel that attempts to limit its harm are more extreme than they actually are.** For example, nonvegans often claim that vegans are extreme merely for not eating animals, and they even question how far a vegan is going to take their veganism each time the vegan extends it to include a new practice, such as not wearing secondhand silk clothing. Similarly, when members of the LGBTQ+ community ask for something as simple yet powerful as changing some of the terminology used in vegan outreach, some vegans complain about "language police" and argue that linguistic changes are being taken too far. In both instances, those with privilege react defensively against practices that reflect evolving consciousness.

Our privilege can reflect badly on us. Regardless of how conscientious a person we know ourselves to be, when we haven't examined our privilege, there is a good chance that we will interact and communicate in ways that cause others to see us as ignorant at best, and bigoted and uncaring at worst. Just think about how your nonvegan uncle comes across when he's arguing with you at the dinner table, insisting that humans would become stupid if they didn't eat animals (since eating animals is supposedly what made our brains grow larger). And consider how a vegan may come across when they promote vegan products as "cruelty-free" even though the manufacturing of such products may have included the exploitation of economically disadvantaged people; or when the vegan claims that becoming literate about "isms" other than carnism and speciesism is a distraction from the "real issue" of helping animals.

Our privilege can harm our relationships. Privilege is nonrelational, in that it causes us to think and act in ways that distance us from our empathy, therefore increasing the likelihood we'll say and do things that hurt others and cause them to feel disconnected from us. For example, how often have you been at a group dinner when someone started teasing you about your veganism, perhaps making "moo" sounds over a steak, or claiming that pigs are meant to be eaten since bacon tastes so good? Chances are the nonvegan has no idea of the extent of anger and perhaps shame you may feel; their carnistic privilege prevents them from being tuned in to your experience. Nevertheless, you likely feel disconnected from them; you feel less safe in their presence and perhaps also find it difficult to maintain respect for them. If this behavior continues, you may become increasingly withdrawn from them. Unexamined privilege can chip away at our relationships, until they die the death of a thousand cuts.

Other forms of privilege, when they remain unexamined, can damage relationships similarly. For example, I recently had dinner with a group of vegan friends, one of whom was a man who shared with us how "impressed" he was that a mutual male friend had begun a relationship with a "hot, much younger woman," and he went into some detail as to why "winning" such a woman was an admirable accomplishment. The women at the table inevitably felt uncomfortable, as they—like virtually all women—had experienced a lifetime of deep and painful conditioning to think of themselves as sexual objects for male gratification, being taught that a central part of their value came from their appearance, their physical beauty and youth. And they were not immune to the epidemic of female self-objectification (perceiving themselves as objects), which women often struggle for years to undo, typically without total success. So many women in the vegan movement (and beyond) have talked to me about the sadness and disappointment and sense of demoralization that gets triggered when they look at themselves through the eyes of men who prize beauty and youth the way they might prize a new car. Our friend was also unaware that his celebration of such female sexuality reflected precisely the kind of thinking that helps drive what is referred to as "rape culture," a culture in which women's (hetero)sexual attractiveness is conflated with their worth and is a key contributor to the fact that women are at high risk of sexual violation. Our friend also didn't realize that his comment was an expression of *ageism*, a prejudice that causes us to devalue, degrade, and discriminate against those who are older (or sometimes younger) than what's widely considered the age ideal.

Our privilege can enable trauma. Powerarchies, from which privilege stems, often cause atrocities, which are mass traumatic events. Those who are oppressed or who witness the oppression often end up traumatized. Just consider the atrocity of carnism and the traumatization of vegans who have witnessed the horrors of the system. Or consider the atrocities committed against women, from legalized sexual slavery to the epidemic of sexual assault in many places in the world, and the traumatization caused by such realities. When trauma is present, normal ways of relating and communicating are often not appropriate or even possible (which is one reason why the #ARMeToo dialogue became so difficult to navigate), and we'll discuss this issue more fully in Chapter 4.

When we understand the ways our unexamined privilege affects others and ourselves, we can appreciate how such privilege not only helps maintain oppressive social dynamics, but also causes interpersonal problems. Vegans of different social groups—white people and BIPOC; men, women, and people of other genders; heterosexual and LGBTQ+ people; and so on—can unknowingly end up engaged in the dysfunctional dynamics of privilege and oppression, dynamics that ultimately disconnect us from one another, diminish morale, and drain energy from the movement. Indeed, because privilege is nonrelational, our unexamined privilege reduces the chances that we will form strong connections within our movement and between our movement and other movements, and it also diminishes our collective integrity, as it can cause us to act against our values of justice and compassion. Our unexamined privilege and the oppression it enables create the very opposite conditions necessary for a unified and empowered movement—a movement that is able to be a true force for animals.

The good news is that our privilege loses much of its power over us once we become aware of it. With awareness, we can change the way we relate within systems of oppression. We can shift from being passive bystanders who help enable oppression to becoming active allies in social transformation. In so doing, we can unify and empower our movement to bring about powerful and lasting change for all beings.

3
Inclusivity Is Strategic
Why We Don't Have to Choose between Being Inclusive and Being Effective

—◦◦◦◦—

Many vegans believe that outreach that's inclusive—outreach that reflects privilege literacy and sensitivity to forms of oppression other than animal oppression—is unstrategic. Most, if not all, vegans who feel this way are those whose privilege literacy is limited. The assumption that we must be strategic *or* inclusive—that we can't be strategic *and* inclusive—is a false dichotomy. In fact, the very opposite is true: our unexamined privilege prevents us from recognizing the strategic importance of inclusivity, causing us to act unstrategically as well as unethically, so that we end up operating in a lose–lose model.

How Being Non-Inclusive Damages the Vegan Movement
The circumstances that led up to #ARMeToo offer a good example of the damage a lack of inclusivity can do to the vegan movement. Unexamined male privilege, and the insensitivity to the oppression of women it causes, created a climate where widespread sexism was the norm (to be sure, sexism is *still* the norm, but post-#ARMeToo

there has been a significant shift of consciousness around the issue). Such a climate is toxic for all involved; as noted, privilege is inherently nonrelational, disconnecting us from one another and causing those who have it to harm those whom it oppresses. In such a climate, true unity among advocates is impossible and the costs of interpersonal dysfunction and injustice siphon much-needed time, energy, and money out of the movement.

The rampant sexism in the movement led to sexual violations, including sexual harassment, which ruined the lives of countless women and drove many committed advocates out of a movement that needs all the help it can get. It also caused significant damage to multiple farmed animal protection organizations. And the more subtle manifestations of sexism, the day-to-day sexist attitudes and behaviors that created a chronically unsafe environment for many women and pushed them to the sidelines of a movement in which they actually make up the majority, was—and is—perhaps no less damaging. Sexism in the movement continues to siphon off a tremendous amount of energy that could otherwise be directed toward helping animals, while preventing women's contributions from being recognized and implemented and destroying morale. (On top of the internal disconnections it causes, sexism in the vegan movement turns off privilege literate nonvegans and prevents the vegan movement from uniting with other social justice movements, such as the feminist movement.)

For example, despite the fact that I'm in a position of leadership in the movement, which affords me authority and provides some protection from sexist attitudes and behaviors, I nonetheless have felt the constant weight of sexism from within (and outside) the movement pulling me down, even as I have striven to be as effective as possible in my advocacy. Like most women, I am no stranger to my sexual boundaries being violated, to being demeaned in a variety of ways because of my gender, to being verbally assaulted for being openly feminist, and also to having to plead and strategize and caretake in the hope of being taken seriously when I share my experiences of, and concerns about, sexism. (One male vegan even said he would "stop [my] feminist rantings at any cost" and threatened to disrupt a talk I was planning to give, which led to me spending the entire event in a state of anxiety, focused less on raising awareness of carnism and more on scanning the crowd.) I have often found myself feeling frustrated, saddened, and demoralized. I can only imagine the impact of such a sexist environment on women who aren't protected by the layers of privilege I have—those not in positions of leadership, or who are women of color, or who are otherwise more vulnerable to the impact of sexism.

In addition to the aforementioned problems, consider the financial cost of sexism to the movement. Dr. Lisa Kemmerer[1] has pointed out that just the legal fees organizations must pay due to sexual harassment charges are tremendous. Add to these expenses the cost of staff time—salaries used for staff to focus their efforts on managing executives' misconduct, involving board members, human resources personnel, public relations and communications officers, and so on. Key staff spend time and money engaged in damage control, managing the problems caused by sexist offenses, rather than doing the work they're funded to do—helping animals.

Sexism is but one example among many of the damage a lack of inclusivity can do to the vegan movement and to the people in it. Such damage is compounded by other powerarchies in the movement, such as racism, classism, and ableism. The price that vegans, and nonhuman animals, pay for enabling these oppressions is incalculable.

---

1 Lisa Kemmerer, "Is Sexism Harming Our Activism for Animals?" YouTube, In Defense of Animals, 5 February 2018, https://www.youtube.com/watch?v=K7EZabfOgs4.

Being Inclusive Doesn't Mean Taking Resources from Animals

A number of vegans believe that being sensitive to oppressions other than the oppression of nonhuman animals in their organizing and outreach would shift resources away from veganism and therefore harm animals. For example, one activist told me, in response to being asked by another activist that their (all-white) group be more racially conscious, "We believe that won't be fair to the animals. There are so few resources for the voiceless that sharing them with all the other 'isms' would be a great injustice."

One reason for this sentiment is that the violence inflicted on animals is so extensive and intensive that it can overshadow that inflicted on other victims of oppression, especially for vegans who aren't well informed about other oppressions. Another reason is that many vegans don't distinguish between *working for* the transformation of other oppressions and *not reinforcing* them. Obviously, any individual only has so much time and energy to dedicate to a cause, and we have to choose which issue we want to focus on. But we can nevertheless work for a particular cause and still commit to not harming others in the process. Consider how some human rights advocates argue that they can't be vegan because they don't have the energy to focus on yet another issue— as though it's not possible to work for human rights and not eat animals in the process. To avoid the same kind of contradiction, vegans can focus their advocacy on nonhuman animal oppression, while also being privilege literate enough not to simultaneously reinforce human oppression.

Being Inclusive Can Expand, Rather than Limit, Our Audience

Sometimes vegans believe that if we are inclusive, our message won't resonate with members of the mainstream and we'll seem even more removed from the norm than we already are. However, being inclusive is not an either/or phenomenon, but a matter of degree: we can aim to be as inclusive as possible, such that we do our very best to avoid reinforcing other oppressions, just as we strive to avoid triggering unnecessary defensiveness in a mainstream audience. Rarely, if ever, is there truly a conflict if we are willing to think creatively and are committed to finding a viable solution.

Furthermore, as marketing experts know, effective outreach is rarely geared toward a wide, general group, such as "the mainstream." Rather, it is focused on specific demographics. Effective vegan outreach is targeted at those who are most allied with veganism—the low-hanging fruits—and those in positions of influence. In terms of the low-hanging fruits, we know that people who constitute this group are socially and politically progressive (and often female),[2] so they are likely to be at least somewhat privilege literate and therefore offended by language and outreach methods that reflect a lack of such awareness. Influencers, which include philanthropic donors, politicians, business leaders, technological innovators, and leaders of other social justice movements, are less homogeneous as a group. Although some influencers are uninformed and unconcerned with issues of privilege and oppression, many hold progressive values, and if we are not inclusive, we risk alienating them. One of the best ways we can deter those in our target demographics from supporting our movement is by coming across as ignorant and bigoted—unaware of, and unconcerned with, any privilege other than human privilege.

2   Niall McCarthy, "Who Are America's Vegans and Vegetarians?" *Forbes*, 6 August 2018, https://www.forbes.com/sites/niallmccarthy/2018/08/06/who-are-americas-vegans-and-vegetarians-infographic/#1dfed940211c; "Humane Research Council, Study of Current and Former Vegetarians and Vegans," 2014, https://faunalytics.org/wp-content/uploads/2015/06/Faunalytics_Current-Former-Vegetarians_Full-Report.pdf; and João Graça, Maria Manuela Calheiros, Abílio Oliveira, and Taciano L. Milfont, "Why Are Women Less Likely to Support Animal Exploitation Than Men? The Mediating Roles of Social Dominance Orientation and Empathy," *Personality and Individual Differences* 129 (July 2018): 66–69.

Our lack of privilege literacy can also make us come across as hypocritical. The "product" our movement is "selling" is values, integrity. So when we promote compassion and justice while seeming to dismiss the experiences and needs of members of oppressed groups in the process, such mixed messaging presents us as ethically inconsistent and, therefore, as untrustworthy and unattractive.

Being Inclusive Helps Target the Roots of Oppression

On a more abstract but no less important level, being inclusive is strategic because it helps ensure that our outreach (and our interpersonal dynamics, as vegan advocates and as people) targets the roots of oppression—powerarchy—rather than just the manifestations of oppression. As noted, the same mentality that enables us to exploit nonhuman beings enables us to exploit human beings. As long as this mentality stays in place, the *content*—the victims of oppression—may change, but the *process*—oppression itself—remains intact. Powerarchy and the oppressive mentality it breeds constantly seek a target, a victim, a morally inferior "other." If we don't shift this mentality, we might liberate farmed animals, but other animals—human or nonhuman—will remain targets for victimization. When our efforts help offset powerarchy (or at least don't reinforce it), we can work toward social transformation on the deepest level, on the level of process.

Being Inclusive Helps Us Think More Creatively and Strategically

When we're inclusive, we're less likely to end up working in homogeneous groups that limit our creative and strategic thinking.[3] Homogeneous groups are made up of people who have

---

3   See Vivian Hunt, et al., "Diversity Matters," McKinsey Report, 2 February 2015, https://assets.mckinsey.com/~/media/857F440109AA4D13A54D9C496D86ED58.ashx.

many of the same ways of processing information, the same cultural language and values, the same types of assumptions, and the same areas in which they're uninformed or unaware. People from diverse backgrounds, on the other hand, bring to the table different ways of thinking and being, and enrich outreach that needs to speak to a diverse audience. For example, white vegan outreach, which focuses largely on consumer choices, doesn't resonate with many BIPOC, whose concerns include systemic injustices in food production and distribution, such as the unavailability of healthy foods in lower-income communities and the exploitative sourcing of foods that harms workers.[4]

Our privilege can keep our analysis shallow, and once we start to think outside the box of privilege, which tends to limit our awareness and stunt our creativity, we can find that there are plenty of powerful ways to conduct vegan outreach that do not require violating anybody. For example, we can design our outreach to ensure that it doesn't include only images and experiences of white people and that it doesn't use male-dominant language or objectify women. These approaches are simple and straightforward and are used by many organizations already. With a commitment to inclusivity, vegan outreach can more fully reflect the compassion and justice our movement is built on.

---

4 For information on food justice and veganism see the Food Empowerment Project at https://foodispower.org; A Well-Fed World at https://awellfedworld.org; and the Vegan Advocacy Initiative at http://veganai.org/.

4
Becoming an Ally

How to Become a Part of the Solution When You're Privileged

———⊷⊶———

Iɴ ᴛʜᴇ ᴘʀᴇᴠɪᴏᴜs chapters, we discussed the basics of what privilege is; how it can affect us as well as others and weaken the vegan movement; and how we can become privilege literate, so that we can more effectively work to create a better world for all beings. In this chapter, we'll discuss some practical steps you can take to become a part of the solution when you're a member of a privileged group.

We don't have control over whether we're privileged or not, since our privilege isn't typically something we can just get rid of. What we do have control over, however, is how we relate to our privilege. As we've discussed, when we are aware of our privilege and its impacts—when we are privilege literate—we can relate to our privilege in a way that offsets, rather than reinforces, oppression. In other words, we can become an *ally* to those who are harmed by and/or are working to transform oppression.

A central aspect of privilege literacy—and therefore of becoming an ally—is knowing how to communicate about our privilege with those who have been harmed by it, so that we can understand why and how to change some of our beliefs and behaviors. Often, our usual ways of communicating are not sufficient. This is largely because those who have been negatively impacted by our privilege may have strong emotions, and possibly even post-traumatic reactions, around the issue. They may have experienced years of oppression, or have been witness to such oppression, and they can, understandably, carry a great deal of pain that's been caused by the damage our privilege has enabled. So they may have strong feelings about our privilege, even if we, ourselves, haven't been direct contributors to the oppression. In order to communicate effectively, then, we first need to appreciate the emotional toll of oppression. We will therefore be less likely to end up misinterpreting reasonable anger as irrational and a legitimate sense of urgency as melodramatic, and communicating in a way that is unproductive or counterproductive.

Appreciating the Emotional Toll of Oppression

Even in their most "benign" forms, oppressive systems chronically disempower those who are disadvantaged and who must live with daily perils, injustices, and affronts to their dignity that are invisible to the privileged and are therefore widely ignored and denied. Often, trauma is also involved: as noted, powerarchies, in their ultimate expression, enable atrocities, or mass traumatic events.

If you're not a member of an overtly oppressed group and can't relate to the experience of disempowerment and traumatization caused by oppression, just think about your experience as a vegan who's witnessed the horrors of carnism, and the justifiable anger and grief you may feel about the oppression of nonhuman animals (and consider how these emotions can become compounded by the fact that your attempts to bring about justice are often met with resistance, hostility, and even mockery). Likewise, members of oppressed groups, who constantly have their experience invalidated by the dominant culture, are often told that their oppression is either not real or as bad as it seems. They are also frequently blamed for the unjust circumstances they find themselves in, learning to believe, for example, that the reason they're not as successful as they could be is that they're just not hardworking, smart, or attractive enough.

Although vegans as a group are not oppressed in the same way as, for example, women, vegans who are not members of overtly oppressed groups can get some understanding of what it feels like to be invalidated by the dominant culture by reflecting on their experience with nonvegans. Nonvegans may deny that carnism is an atrocity, minimize the suffering it causes, and invalidate vegans' message in a variety of ways, often pathologizing vegans as overly emotional or extremist and blaming vegans when vegan advocacy doesn't bring about the desired effect (saying, for example, that the vegan advocate didn't communicate respectfully or rationally enough).

Over time, people who started out simply trying to raise awareness of privilege can end up angry and defensive themselves. When people aren't listened to when they talk, especially about matters where the stakes are high, they often talk louder and eventually end up yelling. Finally, they can fall into despair, as productive conversation seems hopeless.

Understanding Emotional Repression

It's not uncommon for the painful emotions caused by oppression to be stuffed down, or repressed, at least to some degree. People often repress their emotions when they get the message that such emotions are "wrong" (i.e., that what they're emotional about isn't really happening or is their fault) and so they don't feel entitled to feel them. People may also repress their emotions when they believe that it's not safe or useful to feel and express them—when, for example, nobody will take them seriously and they know that they'll end up even more enraged and despairing. Such a dynamic is perhaps easier to understand in the context of a smaller-scale powerarchy, an abusive relationship: as long as the abuser refuses to acknowledge the injustice and harm of their behaviors, the person being abused cannot afford to feel, or to fully feel, their resulting emotions—unless they are ready and able to end the relationship. Repressing emotions in order to function is a coping mechanism that enables people to continue in unhealthy systems they are not free to exit.

Once there is an opening for repressed emotions to emerge, they can come rushing to the surface. This can occur when the denial of those of us who are privileged is pierced and we are finally able to start acknowledging the pain our actions (or the actions of others who share our privilege) have caused. Often at this point, those who have been harmed by our privilege are still reeling from years of emotional (and sometimes physical) wounding—but we are not sufficiently literate and we don't realize that the usual ways of communicating are not appropriate and can even be counterproductive. We discussed how such a phenomenon was played out in the #ARMeToo movement, in which a number of men responded with concern and a genuine desire to engage in productive dialogue, but found that their attempts to do so fueled, rather than offset, the problem.

Stages of Recovery and Appropriate Methods of Communication

Psychologists have noted how recovery from trauma occurs in stages.[1] These stages may also be applicable to recovery from oppression. Understanding these stages can help us recognize how to communicate about our privilege productively.

---

1   See Judith Herman, *Trauma and Recovery: The Aftermath of Violence—From Domestic Abuse to Political Terror* (New York: Basic Books, 2015).

The first stage of recovery is safety. An individual (or group) who has felt unsafe (emotionally or otherwise) and disempowered—hallmarks of both traumatic and oppressive experiences—needs to know, first and foremost, that they won't be further harmed. The second stage is the victim(s) acknowledging and expressing the emotions related to the trauma (which is only possible if safety has been established). In the third and final stage, the victim(s) reconnect with others—and it is only at this point that normal ways of communicating with the victim(s) are appropriate.

When an individual (or group) first begins raising awareness of our privilege, it is not the time to employ our usual means of learning or communicating, such as playing devil's advocate or otherwise second-guessing the validity of what we're being told. Doing so can cause the other to feel that their reality is being denied or to feel otherwise invalidated, mirroring the very methods that had been used to maintain the oppression they're speaking out about. This dynamic was apparent in the #ARMeToo dialogue: many vegan men took to social media in an attempt to join the conversation about sexual harassment in the animal rights movement, but became frustrated at what they believed was an expectation that they stifle their curiosity and suppress their questions, assuming that the current conversation was preventing a diversity of opinions from being shared. But timing matters, and—given that #ARMeToo unfolded during an early stage of recovery (more accurately, #ARMeToo catalyzed the first stage of recovery)—that was not the time for communication as usual.

It is also not the time to question members of oppressed groups' requests for safety measures, such as for creating safe spaces; doing so can come across as further invalidating. Just as we (hopefully) wouldn't argue with a veteran of war who asks us to avoid making sudden loud noises, which can trigger a post-traumatic reaction, neither is it appropriate to argue with a woman who suggests holding a separate forum for women at an animal rights conference. Vegans can perhaps appreciate the need for safe spaces when they consider how much more secure they may feel in a group of their peers who they know won't make offensive comments about eating or killing animals.

It is also not the time for debates or for exploring differences of opinion. These, too, are methods that have been used to invalidate and silence those who are oppressed, and so they can be experienced as triggering and offensive.

Nor is it the time to talk too much about ourselves, including about our own concerns about the problems our privilege has caused. Doing so can be perceived as (and can in fact be) placing ourselves back in the privileged position of being the focus of attention, of being *centered*. Centering ourselves can also be seen as a demand for empathy, and for many people who have been oppressed, empathy for those who have contributed to their oppression (even if such a contribution was not direct or intentional) can be dangerous.

Members of oppressed groups are socialized to over-empathize with members of privileged groups; they often learn to see the world, including themselves, through the eyes of those with privilege and to believe the privileged group's version of reality over their own. And they can perceive their own experiences and needs as less valid than those of the privileged group. (For members of oppressed groups, developing healthy psychological boundaries to avoid over-empathizing with those who have privilege is central to recovery.)

Now is the time to listen—to listen deeply, with the goal of fully understanding the experiences of those who have been oppressed. It is the time to be a compassionate witness, to use the term coined by psychologist Kaethe Weingarten: to listen with empathy, compassion, and without judgment.[2]

There's no set time for how long we should wait before placing ourselves back into the conversation. Once we feel we've listened fully, we can simply ask if it's okay to start sharing our thoughts and feelings. A large part of such interactions is really about feeling them out, doing our best to be present and empathic while appreciating that we'll make mistakes along the way, as none of us is, or should even try to be, perfect.

Steps Toward Becoming an Ally

Following are some practical steps you can take toward becoming an ally:

- **Commit to becoming literate** about systems of oppression and about specific types of privilege. As noted, privilege is typically invisible to those who have it. So don't assume that understanding your human privilege automatically makes you aware of your white or able-bodied privilege.

  Becoming literate isn't simply about reading up on the issues, but rather about truly understanding them, emotionally as well as intellectually. It means looking at the world through the eyes of those who are harmed by your privilege and understanding and empathizing with their experience. Literacy is not just being informed; it's being aware.

  Becoming privilege literate should be something you genuinely want to do so that you can be more of an ally. So if someone offers to share information with you about your

---

2 Kaethe Weingarten, *Common Shock: Witnessing Violence Every Day: How We Are Harmed, How We Can Heal* (New York: Dutton Adult, 2003).

privilege, don't respond by offering a quid pro quo, saying, for example, that you'll learn about white privilege if they read something about how white people are losing social power. This kind of suggestion is both ineffective and offensive, and it wholly denies the literacy gap. Imagine a nonvegan saying they'll read *Animal Liberation* only as long as a vegan reads *The Vegetarian Myth*, as though the vegan hasn't spent a lifetime being spoon-fed carnistic propaganda just like everybody else. The informational playing field isn't level: we all are literate in the dominant way of thinking, since that's what we grew up with. Plus, asking others to expose themselves to information that seeks to justify their oppression or the oppression of those they care about is disrespectful and can be hurtful.

Of course, becoming literate isn't a guarantee that you'll become an ally. Some people become literate about their privilege and still don't care about changing their relationship with it—just as some people learn about the consequences of animal agriculture and don't care about changing their consumption patterns. But if you're reading this book, and you've already chosen to become vegan in order to do less harm in the world, chances are you are indeed concerned about your impact on others and want to become an ally.

- **Take responsibility for your own literacy.** Don't expect others to teach you, which makes them carry the burden of your education.[3] Consider how frustrating it is when

---

3   Aph Ko and Syl Ko, *Aphro-ism: Essays on Pop Culture, Feminism, and Black Veganism from Two Sisters* (Brooklyn, NY: Lantern, 2017). See also Audre Lorde, "The Great American Disease," *Black Scholar* 10, nos. 8/9 (1979): 17–20.

nonvegans expect you to handhold them through their dietary modifications, where you feel like you have to bend over backwards to make eating vegan seem effortless or they'll continue to eat animals. Consider, too, how unfair it feels when the nonvegan expects you to be an expert on everything when you're advocating veganism—of course you don't know all there is to know about vegan nutrition during pregnancy, agricultural economics, veganic farming, and so on. So don't expect those you're talking to about your privilege to have all the answers, either.

- **When your perspective on your privilege differs from the perspective of those who are harmed by it, assume that their perspective is more accurate.** Remember: Our privilege distorts our perceptions while making us believe that we're seeing clearly. And because of the near-universal acceptance of the privileged group's perceptions as fact rather than opinion, our perceptions aren't held to the same standards of accountability as others'. When nearly everyone agrees on something, they are unlikely to feel the need to examine it to ensure that it's actually accurate. For example, when alchemy—the transmuting of metals to treat disease—was the dominant medical model in the Middle Ages, just about everyone believed in the approach, so alchemists weren't held accountable for proving their methods to be effective (which they turned out not to be). It was the chemists—who challenged the alchemist model—who had to prove the accuracy of their approach.

- **Distinguish between accurate and inaccurate sources** of information, as with any educational endeavor. A number of reactionary blogs, books, and films purporting to raise awareness about privilege and oppression, but which actually justify them, are part of a growing backlash against the increasing power of social justice movements; the growth of anti-vegan literature is but one example among many. (In Chapter 1, we discussed ways to determine which sources are trustworthy and there's a list of recommended resources at the end of this book.)

- **Speak out when you hear something oppressive.** If someone says or does something sexist, ableist, racist, or otherwise oppressive, point it out. (We'll discuss how to communicate to challenge privilege in Chapter 5.) If you merely go along to get along, you become a part of the problem, rather than a part of the solution.

- **Support other social justice movements; don't use them.** Supporting another movement means being an ally to the movement and its proponents—using your resources to help them achieve their goals. It does not mean using them to help you achieve your goals.

  Supporting rather than using other social justice movements means, for example, not appropriating hashtags such as #BlackLivesMatter, and repackaging them as #AllLivesMatter. Such appropriation harms both movements. It harms the BLM movement by, for instance, diverting attention from a movement that—for the first time in history—has thrust into the public spotlight the catastrophic injustice that is systemic racism; and by diminishing the gravity of this reckoning. It harms the animal rights movement by making its proponents come across as naïve, unexamined, and opportunistic—as using the momentum created by and for another social justice movement to promote their own message.

This is not to say that the vegan message and movement are not imperative. It is also not to say that forming cross-movement alliances is not important. But when and how to share our message and form alliances matters. Riding on the coattails of others' efforts just when their own movement finally starts to get the attention it deserves is virtually guaranteed to backfire.

- **Don't assume others share your privileges just because they aren't visibly disadvantaged.** Many disadvantages— such as chronic diseases, psychological problems, and socioeconomic status or class—are invisible, so it's essential never to assume that you know what others are capable of or need. Vegan advocate Carolyn Zaikowski[4] explains how it's not uncommon for activists to organize events— such as those that require long bus rides or sleeping in shared and cramped quarters—that are impossible for people with disabilities and older people to attend, and when someone's disadvantage is invisible, they can end up judged for simply trying to take care of their needs. Perhaps the campaigner who doesn't want to sit on a bus for hours has chronic pain, or the activist who chooses not to attend the farmed animal vigil has PTSD, or the staff person at a vegan organization who isn't willing to put in unpaid overtime can't afford to because they don't have

---

4 See Carolyn Zaikowski, "Six Ways Your Social Justice Activism Might Be Ableist," *Everyday Feminism*, 20 (September 2016), https://everydayfeminism.com/2016/09/social-justice-activism-ableist/.

an economic safety net like those who come from more financially advantaged families.

- **If you're in a position of leadership, model a commitment to privilege literacy and inclusivity.** Those heading organizations or groups and those who have a high level of influence in the vegan community have an added responsibility to ensure that they are literate themselves and that they expect literacy among those they influence. If you're in a position of leadership and you choose not to prioritize literacy, you're sending a harmful message to those who look to you as an example.

  Even though leaders[5] can still get away with not being privilege literate, soon enough they won't be able to. The world is rapidly changing and, at some point, those who choose unawareness will be looked upon as having remained willfully ignorant and enabling oppression.

  If you're a leader, you now have the opportunity to be ahead of the curve, putting your forward-thinking approach into action in order to step up and speak out. No matter how busy you are, finding—or, making—the time to become privilege literate may be one of the most important choices you make, for yourself, for the movement, and for the world. You can refer to the resources at the end of this book, and you can also bring in experts who can provide training in diversity and/or bystander intervention for your team. And try to ensure that your organization is diverse, with women, BIPOC, and others who are members

---

5   I'm using the term *leader* simply for the sake of clarity, with the awareness of its limitations—specifically, of the fact that the term can be interpreted as defining someone's character, rather than as referring to a role they are occupying.

of disadvantaged groups adequately represented on your team.

- **Pay attention to some of the specific ways privilege is manifested in your group.** There are some predictable ways privilege shows up in groups. For example, people with privilege tend to take up the space of others, through such actions as interrupting during conversations and talking without pausing to give others the opportunity to participate. They may also be more likely to dismiss feedback before fully considering it and to take credit for others' work. As you become more privilege literate, you will likely begin to automatically recognize such behaviors.

- Similarly, **develop *power literacy*.** Power literacy is understanding the nature and structure of power dynamics and of powerarchy, as well as recognizing how having, or acquiring, even small amounts of power can affect our thoughts and feelings, driving us to engage in abuses of power. Research has shown that when we are in a position of power, we experience diminished empathy; we are less likely to act with integrity; and we are more likely to act in ways that are self-serving, entitled, and impulsive and to justify these behaviors to ourselves and others.[6]

- **When you're working on campaigns or on team projects, make sure that everyone involved has a similar (and sufficient) level of privilege literacy,** or you'll likely end up

---

6   For an overview of power dynamics and powerarchy, see powerarchy.org. And for an excellent examination of the corrupting effects of power, see Dacher Keltner, *The Power Paradox: How We Gain and Lose Power* (New York: Penguin, 2016).

in unproductive debates that both waste time and decrease morale. For example, if you're discussing whether to change your terminology so that it's nonsexist, it's essential that everyone on the team is literate about patriarchy and male privilege. If there are members of the team who have never truly considered or experienced what it feels like to have their gender erased from the language, and who aren't educated about the role language plays in both maintaining and challenging oppression, then they are not in a position to make informed decisions. Giving these individuals such power is like allowing a nonvegan who has little to no understanding of carnism and veganism to share in decision-making for vegan outreach campaigns. Just as it's impossible to have an objective conversation about eating animals as long as we're dialoguing from within the mindset of carnism, it's impossible to have an objective conversation about gender as long as we're operating from within the mindset of patriarchy.

- **Notice your defensiveness, and don't act on it.** If you find yourself feeling defensive—feeling angry, looking for justifications for your privilege, seeking examples to disprove another's perceptions of their experience, minimizing another's experience (such as assuming they're overreacting or exaggerating), not feeling empathy, and so on—consider that it may be your privilege trying to prevent you from evicting it from your consciousness. Try to act in spite of your defensiveness, rather than because of it. (As noted in Chapter 1, your defensiveness may be a reaction to other factors, such as your privilege being challenged in a manner that's not respectful toward you. Try to observe

your internal experience—your thoughts and feelings—
as well as the external dynamic you are engaged in, to
determine the source of your defensiveness. Regardless of
the trigger for your feelings, it's still important that you stay
open to learning about your privilege and about how to be
an ally, even as you might choose to remove yourself from a
particular conversation that doesn't feel safe to continue.)

Changing the way we relate to our privilege and to those who
are disadvantaged by it takes time and effort. We have been deeply
conditioned to relate to others and ourselves in ways that tend to
reinforce, rather than offset, powerarchy. So as we work to break our
patterns, it's important that we are patient with ourselves and not
expect perfection, or immediate transformation. In so doing, we can
practice the same thoughtfulness and compassion toward ourselves
that we're working to bring to our interactions with others.

5
Creating Allies
Communication Strategies for Challenging Privilege

———◦◦◦◦◦———

I N THE PREVIOUS chapter, we discussed how to communicate
when we're in a privileged position and our privilege is being
highlighted or challenged. Now, we'll turn our attention to
examine how we can invite others to become a part of the solution
when we're members, or are speaking out as allies, of an oppressed
group. Specifically, we'll discuss how to communicate in a way
that increases the chances that your message will be heard and
responded to as you intend it to be.[1]

As with any issue, especially one that's sensitive and complex,
privilege needs to be discussed in ways that encourage openness
and enable learning. This is no simple task, since the nature of
privilege is such that it tends to create defensiveness against talking
about it in the first place. And this defensiveness often leads to a
counterproductive dynamic, where the privileged individual or
group resists developing awareness and those challenging the

---

1 Much of the information in this and the following chapter was first published in my
   book *Powerarchy: Understanding the Psychology of Oppression for Social Transformation*
   (Oakland, CA: Berrett-Koehler, 2019).

privilege feel increasingly invalidated, silenced, and frustrated—and then fight harder to break through the defenses.

But fighting defenses rarely works; people typically become even more defensive when they feel attacked. When we try to break down the fortress of privilege by throwing weapons at it, it adapts by becoming stronger. Instead, we need to find the cracks in the fortress and slip through them. We need to reach past, rather than fight against, the fortress—because the fortress of privilege isn't defending a monster; the fortress *is* the monster. We simply need to reach the human mind and heart on the inside of it.

One of the most effective ways to get past the fortress of privilege is to make sure that when we challenge it, we're communicating—to the best of our ability—from a place of mindfulness. That is, we are mindful of what's unfolding in the moment inside and outside of ourselves, and we're not *blended*, or identified with, our anger and pain even as we honor and acknowledge these feelings. We recognize our feelings for what they are: painful emotions that are a normal reaction to witnessing and being harmed by injustice. So we don't mistake our feelings for ourselves, and we don't allow our feelings to create a narrative, or story, in our mind in which we see people as perpetrators, victims, or heroes, with no overlap and no shades of gray. We don't see the privileged individuals as morally inferior, so we don't feel the emotional charge of contempt; we honor the dignity of those whose privilege we are challenging.

Indeed, contempt is a red flag that we've placed ourselves in a position of moral superiority, and this emotion often says more about our own perceptions and attitude than it does about the other. It can be helpful to appreciate that each of us is nothing more nor less than the biology we were born with and every experience we've ever had. Expecting someone to be different from who and how they are is like expecting a tree that's been rained on not to be wet.

When we're more mindful, we're more connected with ourselves and others. We're better able to appreciate nuance and to sense and honor the dignity of others, even as we may hold them accountable and seek to change problematic attitudes and behaviors. We recognize that good people can participate in harmful behaviors, and that individuals are more than just their privilege. So we don't let our emotions override our recognition of our shared humanity.

In order to be able to communicate from a place of mindfulness, timing matters. Everybody needs time to process painful emotions before being able to fully engage with those who have contributed to their pain.

I am not suggesting that we can, or should, remain silent until we're no longer angry. Especially for women, who have been socialized to deny and repress their anger—particularly anger toward patriarchy—it is important to reclaim this emotion. Nor am I suggesting that the responsibility of communicating effectively should be on the shoulders of those who are already carrying the burdens of injustice and suffering caused by privilege. I am simply suggesting that we be mindful of our internal state and consider both the effectiveness and the appropriateness of our communications, which will make us more likely to bring about the kind of change we seek.

Powerful Movements Are Both Disruptive *and* Transformative

Being more mindful increases the chances that our disruptive actions will lead to the positive outcome we desire. Whether we're challenging problematic attitudes and behaviors on the interpersonal level (such as raising awareness of an individual's privilege) or on the collective level (such as challenging systemic oppression), it's important that our efforts are not only disruptive, but also transformative. When we disrupt, we interrupt and challenge the status quo. And when we transform, we change the very nature of the status quo.

Many advocates mistakenly, yet understandably, assume that disruption need not, and often should not, also be transformative. They believe that when it comes to challenging entrenched privilege and patterns of oppression, it's necessary to use name-and-shame tactics and other forms of verbal violence, or the problem they're addressing won't actually be interrupted and halted.

However, proponents of transformative social change, many of whom have been on the frontlines of revolutionary civil rights movements and who follow the Gandhian and Kingian traditions of nonviolence, have long pointed out that it is not only behaviors that must be disrupted, but the violence itself. In other words, true disruption is not about merely ending violent or oppressive behaviors but about disrupting the very mentality that gives rise to those behaviors so that they don't end up becoming reinforced and reproduced. Disruption must be on the level of process, as well as the level of content.

Indeed, as I mentioned in Chapter 1, all forms of oppression and abuse stem from the same nonrelational mentality, and so transforming oppression means shifting this mentality to one that is relational. In his excellent book *Healing Resistance*, longtime organizer and trainer Kazu Haga points out that the vast majority of violence, on both the interpersonal and collective levels, results from trauma, and so ending violence must also entail healing trauma—which, of course, means healing relationships. We cannot hope to heal relationships as long as we continue to engage in behaviors that cause relational harm, such as communications that demean and shame others.

The recommendations in this chapter are not meant to suggest that those of us who are challenging privilege should be passive or placating in our communication, or that we avoid using tactics such as direct action as part of our movement. Nor are they to suggest that we should ever allow harmful behaviors to continue. What I am suggesting is that we work to make sure our actions not only disrupt harm, but also lay the groundwork for healing.

Effective Communication and Leadership

It is particularly important for those in positions of leadership to be mindful of how they communicate, since they're modeling behaviors and influencing the tone of the collective dialogue. This is no small challenge, since leaders of social justice causes often carry the trauma of others; not only have they witnessed the horrors of the oppressive system they're working to transform, but they are frequently the ones to whom survivors turn. So they may have heard story after story of suffering and injustice, and can end up consumed by the pain, looking at the world through the rigid and unnuanced lens of trauma and relating to everyone as though they're either all-good or all-bad, a part of the problem or a part of the solution.

When we communicate in a way that doesn't respect the dignity of those whose privilege we're challenging—even as we may rightfully hold them accountable and call for change—we not only reinforce their defensiveness, we also create defensiveness and fear in those who are observing our behavior. If our efforts to bring about positive change are driven by unprocessed pain, and especially trauma, we risk becoming, and creating, that which we seek to transform (while also reinforcing the toxic moral perfectionism that is unfortunately pervasive in our movement and beyond). We saw some of this destructive communication in the #ARMeToo dialogue, where bullying—character assaults and shaming—was used to show that bullying is wrong. (Ironically, much of this bullying was carried out in the name of feminism, with the— correct—argument that women need to reclaim power. However, feminism is ultimately about *balancing* power, not wielding it over others.) If leaders are not mindful of their approach to challenging privilege, instead of creating a forum for collective healing and a just redistribution of power, they can raise a battle cry that simply feeds the trauma of their base of supporters, reinforcing the very problem they're trying to resolve.

For our communication to be effective, we need to speak to the person, not to their privilege. If people feel that their intrinsic, or fundamental, worth is not being honored—if they feel they are perceived as morally inferior in some way—even if they know that they are being rightfully chastised, they will be less rational and empathic, and therefore less likely to change their problematic attitudes and behaviors.[2] So we need to communicate in a way that is not shaming—that doesn't suggest that the other is morally inferior, or less worthy than we or others are.

Effective Communication Is Not Shaming

A great deal of communication among social change advocates, vegans and nonvegans alike, is shaming. There are several reasons for this.

One reason is that some advocates do indeed assume that those who have not made the same moral choices as they have are somehow morally inferior, and therefore don't deserve to be communicated with compassionately. However, believing that someone's choices, no matter how problematic, means they forfeit their right to being

---

2   See Donna Hicks and Desmond Tutu, *Dignity: The Essential Role It Plays in Resolving Conflict in Our Lives and Relationships* (New Haven, CT: Yale University Press, 2011).

treated with respect is precisely the kind of thinking that caused the problem such communication is attempting to change.

Another reason we may shame others is that most of us never learned how to communicate effectively. That is, we haven't learned the skills that would help us communicate in a way that reflects the integrity we may be trying to inspire in those with whom we're dialoguing.

Moreover, we often mistake someone's privilege for who they are; we fail to recognize that people are more than just their privilege. In addition, when we're interacting with people who are in positions of power—which includes being in a position of privilege—it's easy to forget that they, like everyone, have vulnerabilities. We often assume that there's an inverse relationship between power and vulnerability—that the more power someone has, the less vulnerable they feel. This is often not the case, and sometimes the opposite is true. Often, critics who publicly shame celebrities, and employees who talk degradingly about their supervisors, do so because they assume that the powerholders are somehow immune to such attacks. However, virtually nobody is immune to the toxic and debilitating effects of shame.

The final reason so many advocates use shame as a tactic is because they believe—incorrectly—that shame will motivate people to change. In fact, one of the best ways to *de*motivate people to change is to shame them. Shame is so disruptive to our sense of self, and so painful an emotion, that most people react to being shamed by withdrawing or attacking in self-defense. Shamed people typically do not feel the esteem or confidence necessary to open themselves up to potentially painful truths about their participation in injustice and to take positive action on others' or their own behalf. Instead, they encase themselves in the emotional armor necessary to prevent further shaming. Although some people claim that they were inspired to change by having been shamed, it is likely that they changed in spite of the shaming, rather than because of it. Studies have shown that shaming behaviors—which are those that harm dignity—trigger a defensive response that reduces the likelihood a person will be open to making positive changes.[3] So if we want people to be open to a message, especially one that challenges their self-concept as an ethical person, we would do well not to water the seeds of shame, which will more likely cause that person to feel disconnected from us and fearful of being further shamed.

Those who are privilege literate know that the "fragility" of people whose privilege is being challenged—the heightened sensitivity to shame they feel—can sometimes be a way for them to avoid accountability or an excuse not to discuss the issue. I'm not suggesting that we enable such fragility, or coddle defensiveness, but simply that we practice respectful, compassionate communication (which is necessary for all communications, not only those about privilege).

Of course, people can feel shamed even if we're not communicating in a shaming manner. But that doesn't change the fact that we're responsible for our own part in a communication. Below are some practical tips for how to talk about privilege in a way that is empowering, rather than shaming:

- **Don't assume you know the internal experience of the privileged person(s)** you're communicating with or about. Don't, for example, assume that you know why they said or did something insensitive—such as assuming that it's because they just don't care or they're selfish. Allowing others to be the expert on their own experience is a generosity we

3   Richard G. Erskine, "Shame and Self-Righteousness: Transactional Analysis Perspectives and Clinical Interventions," *Transactional Analysis Journal* 24, no. 2 (1994): 86–102.

all deserve and is the opposite of the nonrelational attitude that reflects privilege.

- **Avoid character assassination.** Calling someone a sexist because they made a comment that is sexist is conflating one's character (which we can't know since we're not in their mind) with their behavior—and it's more likely to turn people off to a cause than to win supporters to it.

- **Speak to the person, not to their privilege, assuming goodwill.** It can help to remember that people are more than just their privilege and "good" people engage in harmful behaviors and that doesn't make them "bad." As noted, believing that engaging in problematic behavior means someone forfeits their right to be treated with basic respect is precisely the kind of thinking that caused the problem our communication is attempting to change.

- **Remember our bond as vegans.** It takes tremendous courage and conviction to live our truth as vegans in a dominant, animal-eating culture that daily offends some of our deepest sensibilities and that is a constant source of stress with which we must contend. We have to live with the awareness of the horrific suffering going on all around us, all the time; we carry this burden of knowing wherever we go. We are often the lone vegan in groups and communities, left to defend ourselves and our way of life as we're mocked for our caring and rejected for our beliefs. Only another vegan knows what it is to be awake in such a way, in the midst of a global atrocity the rest of the world denies and perpetuates. This knowing, and caring, is a powerful bond we share. When we're frustrated by our differences, struggling to communicate about problems such as privilege and oppression in our movement, it can help to remember, and honor, our bond as vegans, and to remember that we all want to help create a better world.

- **Focus your communication on observable behaviors, not on your interpretations of the behaviors.** For example, rather than say, "He made a sexist comment and won't respond to my criticism about it, so that means he wants to hold onto the power that comes with his male privilege," simply focus on the comment and the fact that the person didn't respond.

- **Stay connected with your empathy.** When you're discussing someone's privilege, be careful to consider how your feedback will feel to them. Imagine them reading what you write or hearing what you say and frame your message in a way that's respectful of their dignity, even as you point out the problems their privilege causes. If you feel unsafe remaining empathic, worrying that you'll lose your own perspective if you are too open to the other's, then you might need more time to heal and shore up your psychological boundaries before speaking out about the issue.

- **Avoid absolutes** (e.g., all vegans, all men), which are rarely accurate and come across as blaming all people for the actions of some.

- **Stick to the facts.** Avoid hyperbole, and communicate the facts as objectively as possible. For example, don't refer to someone's comments that offended you as "cruel statements." You can't know the intention of the speaker (unless they've told you) so you can't know if the statements were intended to harm. Instead, you can say, "statements that offended me" or "statements that I found offensive."

- **Be wary of the tendency to wrap disrespectful communication within intellectual critique.** It's not uncommon for disrespectful communication to be hidden beneath academic rhetoric—especially when it comes to critiquing others' ideas—and the scholarly nature of such critique along with the complex sentences and vocabulary make the disrespect difficult to detect. Even intellectual critiques can, and should, reflect compassion. (And ideally, critiquing others' ideas should not be done via social media, which is not an appropriate platform for thoughtful discussion.)

- **When feasible, communicate with an individual privately, rather than in public.** Of course, there are times when publicly pointing out someone's privileged behavior can be useful—such as when the person is a celebrity and is not personally accessible, or when it's necessary to publicly counter a problematic message they're communicating, or when they've engaged in bullying or violent behavior such as sexual harassment and they pose a threat to others or to the integrity of the group impacted (as we've seen with #MeToo). However, many people who make offensive statements are simply unaware of their privilege and end up being publicly reprimanded, when sharing critical feedback in private would be both more respectful and likely more strategic, since it doesn't make you come across as insensitive. Regardless of whether you are giving feedback privately or publicly, it's important to communicate respectfully. "Call-out culture"[4] has become problematic in that it often involves exposing and punishing misdeeds rather than truly raising awareness and inspiring change. We are unlikely to win allies by calling people out; inviting people into dialogue[5] is often a more effective approach. Calling people out also sends a message to others that they are at risk of being publicly shamed, and they, too, are at risk of character assassination and less likely to engage in a productive dialogue about privilege and oppression.

- **Don't use empowering concepts and terms to reinforce oppressive dynamics.** A number of concepts and terms have emerged in order to highlight and challenge the defensiveness caused by privilege. However, although these expressions can be valuable means to initiate productive conversations, when they are not used accurately or respectfully, they can end up instead creating destructive dialogue, often causing those who are being asked to change their relationship with their privilege to feel they are in a no-win situation. For instance, if a privileged person doesn't speak out in an online discussion about oppression, they may be told they're hiding behind their privilege and not an ally. If they do speak out—even if

---

4 The notion of calling out originated in Black social justice circles, as an important way to challenge racism by naming oppressive behaviors and policies and holding the offending individuals and institutions accountable. However, the practice of calling out has become mainstreamed, and it is not always used toward its original ends.

5 See Ngọc Loan Trần, "Calling IN: A Less Disposable Way of Holding Each Other Accountable," *Black Girl Dangerous*, 18 December 2013, http://www.bgdblog. org/2013/12/calling-less-disposable-way-holding-accountable/.

they make it clear they're speaking from the only position they can, their own experience—they may be told they're centering themselves or, worse, erasing the voices of those with less power, and that they shouldn't be speaking. If, when they speak out, they make a comment that reflects an ignorance of their privilege, as all of us inevitably do, their character may be attacked (they may be called "racist," "sexist," "ableist," and so on). If they feel ashamed or hurt, they may be told they are "crying male tears" (that their shame is exaggerated or fabricated). If they explain their reasoning for an opinion or statement, they may be told they're being defensive. If they've been on the receiving end of disrespectful, inflammatory comments and they ask to be spoken to respectfully, they may be told they're tone policing. (Note that tone policing is stating that one should not communicate when feeling or expressing emotion; this is not the same as requesting that communication be respectful, which is healthful and necessary for productive conversation.) So we need to remember to allow others to be the experts on their own experience, lest we communicate (and send a message to onlookers) that defining someone's reality, or dictating what is true for another individual, and making disrespectful comments are acceptable behaviors toward those we disagree with—and lest we use the tools that were constructed to transform oppression to instead reinforce it.

- **Make sure your facts are accurate.** There are countless examples on social media of comments that appear to reflect unexamined privilege but have been taken out of context or misconstrued. Such a lack of attentiveness can devastate the people whose words or actions are being publicly displayed. I have personally seen grown men—including those in positions of top leadership—cry openly after witnessing online commentaries in which their words were misapprehended and they were portrayed as uncaring or otherwise unethical.

- **Avoid sharing (or making) comments that are disrespectful or otherwise shaming.** This includes comments that convey yelling (such as using all capital letters and exclamation points). Toxic, or unkind and disrespectful, communication is epidemic in large part because the people propagating it are not held accountable, often because we believe their ends (e.g., social justice) justify their means. Be extremely skeptical of anyone who claims that it's ever appropriate to communicate without compassion and respect. One way to recognize oppressive, powerarchical thinking in yourself is to ask yourself whether you're perceiving another as morally inferior, and if you're feeling the corresponding emotion of contempt.

- **Make sure the goal of your commentary is to raise awareness and bring about positive change.** If your goal is to be right or to express your anger, your communication will no doubt reflect this fact and be unproductive or counterproductive. Of course, you *may* be right, and you may well have a right to be angry. It's simply important that these feelings not be ends in themselves.

- **Appreciate that vegan organizations are made up of vegan people**—people who often are strongly identified with and care deeply about the organization. So all of the guidelines in this section apply to communicating about organizations.

It's easy to assume that organizations are unfeeling, abstract entities and thus it is acceptable to communicate harshly about them. It's also easy to assume that the leaders of those organizations have a level of power that protects them from being harmed by disrespectful communications. However, organizations are made up of people—vegan people in this case—who have chosen to dedicate their lives to ending the bloodshed of carnism. Don't assume that these people, including (and often especially) the organizational leaders, don't struggle just like you may to feel that they're doing enough to help animals. Don't assume they don't lie awake at night haunted by images of tortured animals. Don't assume they aren't already trying their best to manage their own shame around not being a "good enough" person, like most of us do. Organizations don't read or hear communications; the people running them do. Be just as sensitive in your communications about organizations as you are in your communications about individuals.

- **Remember that an inverted powerarchy is still a powerarchy.** Of course, societal powerarchies, such as patriarchy and speciesism, clearly cause far more harm than smaller-scale ones. Nevertheless, all powerarchies cause harm. So it's important to remember that even if your goal is to bring about positive change, if you engage in behaviors that violate integrity and harm dignity there's a good chance you'll just create more of the same.

*

At the beginning of this book, I explained that, although the vegan movement is in some ways flourishing, it is also fractured. Unexamined privilege among many vegans has caused the movement to be less unified and powerful than it could otherwise be, and communication about the issue, which is central to healing and creating more unity, has often reinforced rather than mitigated the problem.

As with all problems, from the mundane to those threatening the very existence of the planet, awareness is a key to transformation. When we are aware of oppressive systems and the privileges they create, we can change how we relate within those systems. We can, as noted, become active agents of transformation rather than passive bystanders who reinforce oppression. And when we understand the principles of effective communication, we can challenge privilege in a way that increases the likelihood that our message will be heard and heeded.

With awareness, we can be begin to unmerge our consciousness from the influence of destructive matrices and help create a more unified and effective movement. So not only can we repair our movement, we can help it grow stronger. When we are willing to do the messy and sometimes painful work of peering into the darkness of the fractures in our movement and see our own role in sustaining these cracks, we can emerge with greater wisdom and empowerment. As Ernest Hemingway wrote, "The world breaks everyone and afterward many are strong at the broken places."

I wrote this book to help us become strong at the broken places: for our movement, ourselves, and our world. And for the nonhuman animals, who deserve nothing less.

Afterword

Christopher Sebastian

———◆◇◆———

M Y FIRST EXPOSURE to the word *privilege* in social justice discourse was Peggy McIntosh's classic paper, "White Privilege: Unpacking the Invisible Knapsack." Although that paper has been around since 1988, it was not until circa 2014 that someone shared it in my own circle of acquaintances. I was peripherally aware that white people benefitted from a system of unearned advantages due to their race, but I was excited to finally have the language to describe something that was so real and yet so intangible.

I quickly jumped down the rabbit hole that introduced me to such scholars as Kimberlé Crenshaw and Patricia Hill Collins. Soon my online and offline conversations were filled with the rich language of intersectionality and all the concepts that came along with it.

Of course, as with all things, I was gradually confronted with the limitations of how I, and others, applied (or misapplied) our newfound knowledge. Eventually, I sought to express myself without using the term *privilege*.

I decided that privilege as a standalone concept was flawed. Too many of us treat privilege like a bank. If you're white, you have XXX privilege dollars. If you're male, you have XXX privilege dollars. If you're white **and** male, you've doubled your currency!

On the flip side, if you're Black, female, and even disabled (if you really want to add the old razzle dazzle), then your balance hovers at the low water mark. And if you're an animal (whom our society devalues to the point of not even considering them to be an oppressed class), then your balance has plunged deep into the negative.

In our collective haste to use privilege as a trading commodity on the social justice stock market, many of us have turned it into a zero-sum game. Discussions around it have become frustrated by seeking ways to avoid accountability for our own privilege by pointing out the areas where we are not. It has become a weapon to brandish during debate, a way to dismiss critical discourse. You can be absolved of the privilege of being male and cisgender if you point out that you're disabled and poor. Few of us are universally privileged, and few of us are universally oppressed. But using privilege in this way frames it as a failure of the individual, and it obscures systemic oppression.

The rallying cry of "check your privilege" demands little of the participants. Telling someone to do so all too often ends discussions instead of expanding them. When we compartmentalize our experiences based strictly on one-dimensional aspects of our identities, the system itself is rendered invisible.

Acknowledging our own privilege or encouraging others to locate theirs can be a great starting point. But when it comes to meaningful social change, it is not enough.

Enter *The Vegan Matrix*. This book puts privilege back on the menu for some people in a big way. It is an easy primer for people unfamiliar with social justice jargon to learn about privilege through clear examples, and it provides easy references to people who want to learn more. *The Vegan Matrix* does not **replace** existing literature; it introduces the uninitiated vegan to experts when that reader is ready to take a deep dive.

Most importantly, however, the book gives us ideas on what we can **do** with our privilege, and also how we can talk about privilege—how we can challenge others' privilege in a way that opens up productive conversation rather than creating more defensive debates. *Matrix* gives readers practical tools to challenge institutional violence through building awareness and practicing effective communication. Mind you, *Matrix* does not seek to instruct. The path to tackling systemic oppression is too winding and varied. There is no obvious roadmap to ending intermingled injustice. If there were, we would have followed it and lived happily ever after.

But no. This book seeks to educate. It allows us to view and internalize experiences from perspectives we haven't considered. And that is a valuable step along the path to collective liberation and how far we have to travel **together**.

Recommended Resources

PLEASE NOTE THAT these lists are far from comprehensive. To avoid overwhelming readers, I have listed only a small handful of recommendations.

General Books
The most reliable and comprehensive books for learning about privilege and oppression are classified as textbooks, meaning that they are marketed primarily to educators and they are more expensive than other books. I have listed the most reader-friendly and comprehensive ones that I know of. If you want to choose only one book to read, I recommend either the first or second one, each of which provides the most comprehensive and accessible overview of the subject.

1. *The Psychology of Oppression* by E. J. R. David and Annie O. Derthick (New York: Springer, 2017) covers pretty much all the basic, necessary-to-know information about privilege and oppression and is comprehensive yet not terribly long.
2. *Readings for Diversity and Social Justice* edited by Maurianne Adams, et al. (London: Routledge, 2013) provides a comprehensive yet easy-to-read overview of privilege and

oppression and includes essays on specific forms of oppression. The newest and most up-to-date version is more expensive, but there are older and more affordable editions available for purchase online.

3. My book *Powerarchy: Understanding the Psychology of Oppression for Social Transformation* (Oakland, CA: Berrett-Koehler, 2019) is about the common mentality and structure that drives all oppressive systems. You can also find information about powerarchy at powerarchy.org.

4. *The Gender Knot: Unraveling the Patriarchal Legacy* by Allan G. Johnson (Philadelphia: Temple University Press, 1997) gives an excellent overview of gender dynamics. Johnson also wrote a shorter book, *Privilege, Power and Difference* (New York: McGraw Hill, 2005) that gives an overview of privilege and oppression in general—though this book is less comprehensive than the other books listed on the subject. Johnson's blog (www.agjohnson.us/essays) includes essays on patriarchy, racism, and other forms of oppression.

5. *Privilege: A Reader* edited by Michael S. Kimmel and Abby L. Ferber (New York, Routledge, 2018) is said to be an excellent introduction for those who wish to explore the dynamics of privilege and oppression. Unlike the other books listed here, I have not read this one myself.

Other Books and Blogs

1. For those who feel thrown into new territory, you can start out by taking a look at "Privilege 101: A Quick and Dirty Guide," a blog by Sian Ferguson on *Everyday Feminism* (September 29, 2014). It will give you an overview of the concept of privilege, and other essays on the blog explore related issues.

2. Also on *Everyday Feminism*, you'll find "6 Ways Your Social Justice Activism Might Be Ableist," by vegan advocate Carolyn Zaikowski (September 20, 2016). This excellent article explains how social justice activists often unknowingly engage in ableism.

3. Aph and Syl Ko's brilliant essays on the ways racism, speciesism, and sexism interconnect can be read in *Aphro-ism: Essays on Pop Culture, Feminism, and Black Veganism from Two Sisters* (Brooklyn, NY: Lantern, 2017).

4. Dr. A. Breeze Harper has done groundbreaking work examining the interconnectedness of oppressions. Her work can be found at www.sistahvegan.com.

5. "Class Privilege 101," Rita Rathbone's article on classism at *Have You Heard* (August 11, 2016), explains some of the ways class privilege can manifest (the article is focused on the U.S., but a number of the concepts apply beyond the U.S.).

6. *Veganism in an Oppressive World: A Vegans-of-Color Community Project* edited by Julia Feliz Brueck (Sanctuary Publishers, 2017) is an accessible volume of writings about how to create a more inclusive vegan movement.

7. *Healing Resistance: A Radically Different Response to Harm* by Kazu Haga (Berkeley, CA: Parallax Press, 2020) provides an insightful and powerful explanation of why and how to use Kingian nonviolence to work toward social and personal transformation.

8. *Getting Relationships Right: How to Build Resilience and Thrive in Life, Love, and Work (Oakland, CA: Berrett-Koehler, 2020)* is the book I wrote to promote relational literacy, which helps offset oppressive and abusive attitudes and behaviors. The book provides the necessary information to help readers cultivate healthy relational dynamics—including power dynamics—and effective communication.

9. *Beyond Beliefs: A Guide to Improving Relationships and Communication Among Vegans, Vegetarians, and Meat Eaters* (Brooklyn, NY: Lantern, 2017) is another book I wrote, which is similar to *Getting Relationships Right* except that it's geared toward vegans.

Videos

1. Lisa Kemmerer is a leading feminist in the vegan movement. An excellent video of a webinar she gave about sexism in the movement, entitled "Is Sexism Harming Our Activism for Animals?" (February 5, 2018), is available on YouTube.

2. By shedding light on various oppressions in his talk "Intersections of Justice: Building an Inclusive Animal Rights Movement" (March 26, 2016), vegan and social justice advocate Christopher Sebastian examines and calls for inclusivity in the animal rights movement. The video is available on YouTube.

3. Ashton Applewhite's excellent talk on ageism, "Let's End Ageism" (April 2017) is available on the TED Talk website (www.ted.com).

4. For a wonderful presentation on racism, I recommend watching Tricia Rose's talk, "How Structural Racism Works," presented at Brown University on June 27, 2017.

Relevant Organizations

1. The Food Empowerment Project (www.foodispower.org) encourages healthy food choices that can help cultivate a more compassionate society, by spotlighting the abuse of animals on farms; the depletion of natural resources; unfair working conditions for produce workers; and the unavailability of healthy foods in low-income areas.

2. <u>A Well-Fed World</u> (awfw.org) is a hunger relief and environmental advocacy organization that seeks to reduce the human and animal suffering caused by carnism.

3. <u>Encompass</u> (encompassmovement.org) seeks to increase effectiveness in the animal protection movement by fostering greater racial diversity, equity, and inclusion while empowering advocates of color.

4. <u>CANHAD</u> (www.canhad.org) aims to empower animal, environmental, and human rights advocates to fight harassment and discrimination in advocacy organizations.

About the Author

—◇◇◇◇—

MELANIE JOY, PhD, is a psychologist, international speaker, and longtime vegan and social justice advocate. She is the award-winning author of six books, including *Why We Love Dogs, Eat Pigs, and Wear Cows: An Introduction to Carnism*; *Beyond Beliefs: A Guide to Improving Relationships and Communication for Vegans, Vegetarians, and Meat Eaters*; *Powerarchy: Understanding the Psychology of Oppression for Social Transformation*; and *Getting Relationships Right*. Joy taught courses on privilege and oppression at the University of Massachusetts, Boston for over a decade, and she is the eighth recipient of the Ahimsa Award—previously given to the Dalai Lama and Nelson Mandela—for her work on global nonviolence. Her work has been featured in major media outlets around the world, and she is the founding president of Beyond Carnism. You can learn more about her at carnism.org.

About the Publisher

———◦◦◦———

LANTERN PUBLISHING & MEDIA was founded in 2020 to follow and expand on the legacy of Lantern Books—a publishing company started in 1999 on the principles of living with a greater depth and commitment to the preservation of the natural world. Like its predecessor, Lantern Publishing & Media produces books on animal advocacy, veganism, religion, social justice, and psychology and family therapy. Lantern is dedicated to printing in the United States on recycled paper and saving resources in our day-to-day operations. Our titles are also available as e-books and audiobooks.

To catch up on Lantern's publishing program, visit us at www.lanternpm.org.

facebook.com/lanternpm
twitter.com/lanternpm
instagram.com/lanternpm